MicroAliens

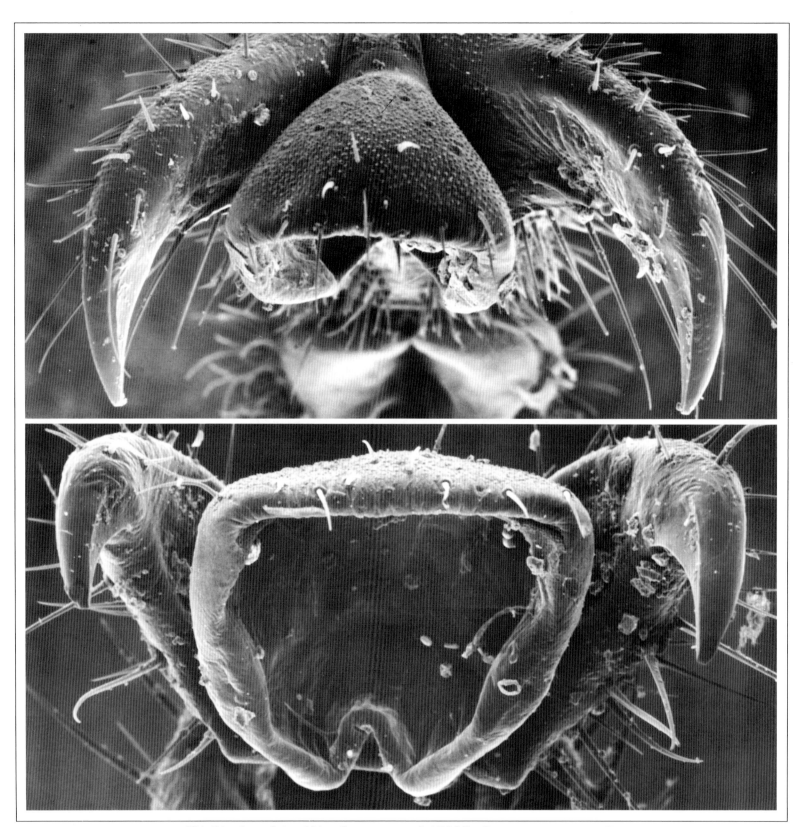

This thing is good at grabbing. Can you guess what it is? For the answer, turn to page 78.

MicroAliens

Dazzling Journeys with an Electron Microscope

Howard Tomb and Dennis Kunkel

with drawings by Tracy Dockray

SCHOLASTIC INC.

New York   Toronto   London   Auckland   Sydney

For Sam James
H.T.

and for Nancy
D.K.

Text copyright © 1993 by Howard Tomb.
Photographs copyright © 1993 by Dennis Kunkel.
Drawings copyright © 1993 by Tracy Dockray.
All rights reserved. Published by Scholastic Inc., 555 Broadway,
New York, NY 10012, by arrangement with Farrar, Straus and Giroux.
Designed by Charlotte Staub.
Cover photographs colorized by Joe Wilmhoff.
Cover design by Charlotte Staub and Lilian Rosenstreich.
Printed in the U.S.A.
ISBN 0-590-48596-2

2   3   4   5   6   7   8   9   10   14   01   00   99   98   97   96   95   94

Contents

The Electron Microscope 6

The Electron Microscope

In 1674, a Dutch scientist named Antonie van Leeuwenhoek (LAY-van-hoke) built a microscope more powerful than any built before. Looking through his new microscope at a drop of water, he saw tiny blobs changing shape and swimming with tiny arms.

It was almost as if Leeuwenhoek had discovered an alien world. He was the first person to see that millions of strange creatures live all around and inside us. Like us, they grow, move around, look for food and places to live, and eventually die. But without a microscope, these alien creatures are invisible.

Leeuwenhoek's microscopes were early versions of the optical or light microscope, the modern version of which you might have in your science classroom or at home. With his microscopes, Leeuwenhoek was able to see things nobody had even imagined, including the cells of the human body. His discoveries changed the way we see the world.

Following his lead, people built better light microscopes and further explored the microscopic world. But scientists soon realized that the amount of detail that can be seen with a light microscope is limited. In the light microscope, an object is magnified by glass lenses bending light rays coming from the object. A light microscope can show only things large enough to bend or refract light rays. Some objects or details of objects are too small to do so.

Early in this century, scientists studying electricity learned that a stream of electrons has a much shorter wavelength than a beam of light and interacts with things too tiny to deflect a beam of light.

Electrons are electrically charged particles, smaller than atoms, which can be made to flow in a stream. Electrons flow through wires into our houses —we call that flow electricity. Because electrons have a negative electric charge, they are attracted to and repelled by magnets. In an electron microscope, magnetic "lenses" deflect an electron stream, shot from an electron gun, directing and focusing the beam on the specimen.

The first *transmission* electron microscope (TEM), built in 1931 by German scientists, enlarged things up to one million times. But the TEM can only shoot electrons through a slice of material, and the slice must be so tiny that scientists use a cutting tool with a sliver of diamond for a blade. The result is a very flat-looking image.

The first *scanning* electron microscope (SEM) was made in 1935, also in Germany. Dennis Kunkel, who took the pictures in this book, uses a modern and much more advanced SEM. It can magnify things up to about 200,000 times actual size. Unlike a light microscope, an SEM can show clear surface details at both high and low magnifications.

Dennis dries specimens and then coats them with a microthin layer of gold. He mounts them in a chamber beneath the electron gun of the SEM. After he closes the door on the chamber, the air is sucked out

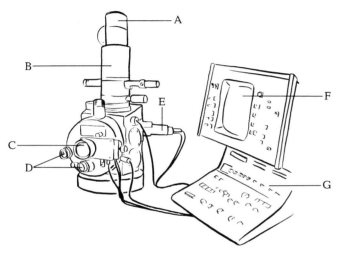

A. Electron gun   B. Air-free column with scanning magnets and magnetic lenses   C. Specimen chamber   D. Controls for moving specimen under beam   E. Electron detector, collector, and amplifier, with cable to viewing screen   F. Viewing screen   G. Controls for adjusting focus and magnification

with a vacuum pump, since air particles prevent electrons from moving freely.

When Dennis turns on the electron beam, which is less than a millionth of an inch wide, it "scans" back and forth across the specimen, knocking electrons off the gold. These electrons are collected and then converted into an electronic signal that is sent to a screen, like the one on a television set, where Dennis can view or photograph the image.

An SEM reveals the fine details of three-dimensional objects. Entire specimens—not just slices of them—are in focus, revealing more than ever about the microscopic world.

Electrons, unlike light waves, don't produce color. That's why all SEM pictures are taken in black-and-white. Colors can be added later with a paintbrush or a computer, as on the cover of this book, but to see true colors, you need a light microscope.

Scientists use scanning electron microscopes to look at plants, insects, people, food, diseases, fossils, metals, and even shampoo. They discover new things all the time, and with each discovery come new questions.

To find the answers, and to ask more questions, we need new scientists. Will you be one of them?

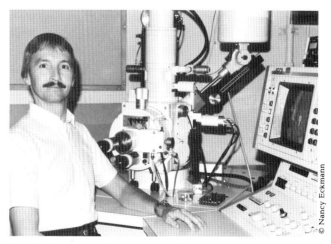

Dennis Kunkel at the scanning electron microscope.

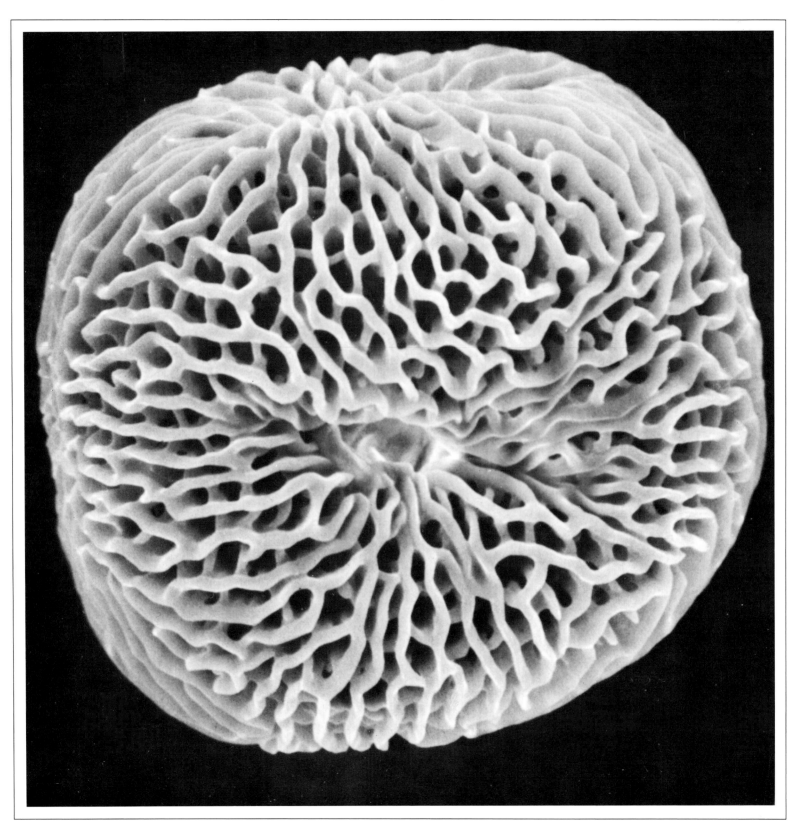

Inside this beautiful box is a coded message. Can you guess what it is? See page 78 for the answer.

The Air

Sometimes when you look at a sunbeam slanting into a room you can see that air is crowded with tiny particles. And when you watch a dog sniff the air or an ant wave its antennae around, you can tell the air carries more than dust. It is full of living things and their messages.

BEES

All honeybee workers are female. Male bees, or drones, never work—their only duty is to mate. A worker visits flowers to drink nectar and collect pollen. She stores the nectar in a special "honey stomach" and passes it through her tongue, or proboscis, to other workers when she returns to the hive. The workers turn nectar into honey by mixing it with invertase, a chemical from their bodies. They keep honey in a wax honeycomb, capped for storage.

When bees are hungry, they eat from the waxy "honeypots" in the hive. Bees also feed honey to larvae, the developing bees, which look like small white legless caterpillars as they grow in the hive.

Besides honey, larvae also eat pollen. As workers collect pollen, they fertilize flowers by carrying grains of pollen from one flower to the next. Bees are so good at this—and so good at making honey—that people have raised them for more than four thousand years. Many farmers rely on bees to pollinate their crops. And before we learned to make sugar a few hundred years ago, honey was the sweetest thing we knew.

Honeybees may join you at a picnic because soda pop and fruit juice are sweet enough to be made into honey. If a honeybee finds enough sweet liquids at your picnic, she may do a special, wiggly dance when she gets back to the hive, to tell the other bees where to find you.

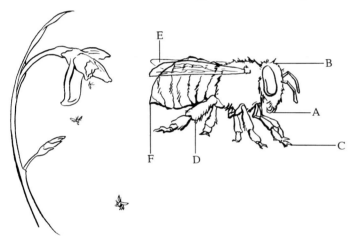

Proboscis (X34, or 34 times larger than actual size). *Every animal has a mouth suitable for the food it eats. A honeybee has a flexible proboscis with a furry tip that sops up nectar like a tiny paintbrush.*

You might see bees drinking water. They mix water with honey because pure honey is too thick and sticky to feed to larvae.

During hot weather, bees collect water to cool the hive. A worker will drink water and, using her proboscis like a wand, make a tiny bubble. Standing at the hive entrance, the bee will then fan her wings on the bubble to blow cool air into the hive.

The tube running along this bee's proboscis is very fragile. The tip of the tube looks jagged in the picture—it may have been broken when Dennis prepared the bee for the SEM.

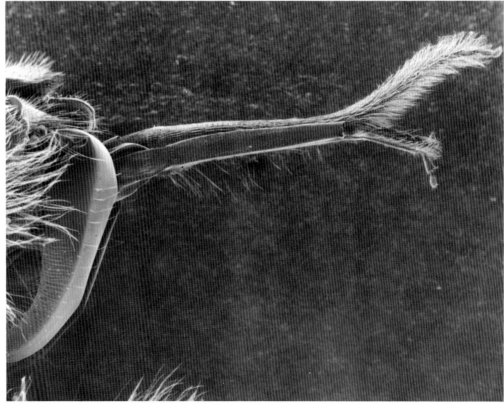

A

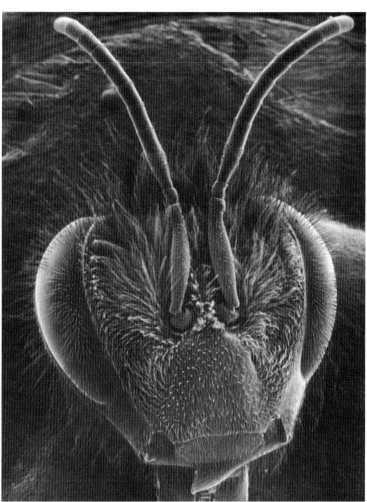

Head (X22). *A honeybee may visit several hundred flowers on one trip. Unlike insects such as ants, bees need large eyes to find food.*

Bees have hairs between the facets, or lenses, of their eyes for the same reason we have eyelashes—to protect the eyes and keep dust away. Some of the hairs are attached to nerves inside the bee's body, so it can feel the wind and flowers it visits. The bee's outer shell, called an exoskeleton, is hard and has no feeling.

The exoskeleton cannot stretch like skin, so an insect must molt, or shed it, to grow. A bee, though, does not molt again after reaching adulthood.

B

C

Claw (X157). *Each worker bee has special claws and brushes on her front legs which she uses to comb pollen from her body to the pollen baskets on her back legs. You can see how the bottom edge of the bee's leg would make a good brush.*

Pollen basket (X1,060). *The bee combs pollen between the stiff, curved hairs that grow in rows on the outside surface of her back legs. One worker may collect millions of pollen grains in a single trip. Even so, feeding a single hungry larva may take ten trips.*

D

11

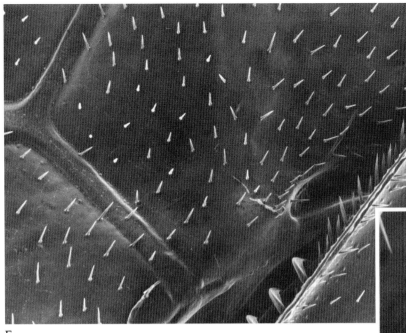

E

Wing (X165). *Bees have no muscles in their wings— their leg and wing muscles are inside their thorax, the body section between the head and the abdomen.*

The veins in a wing, the raised lines you see here, are stiff, like battens in a sail, to keep the wing from bending or twisting.

Wing hooks (X308). *For high-speed flying, up to fifteen miles per hour, the leading edge of the back wings are attached to the trailing edge of the front wings with special hooks.*

If you try to swat a bee, it can unhook its wings to work independently of one another, allowing it to do tricky maneuvers—and even fly backward.

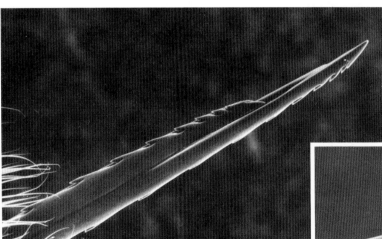

Barbs (X1,485). *When a honeybee stings a person or another animal, the stinger's barbs may catch under the skin, pulling the stinger and venom sac out of the bee's body.*

After a bee sting, you may see the venom sac sticking out of the wound in your skin. The sac may continue to pump venom into the wound through the hollow stinger.

After losing its stinger, a honeybee will eventually die from the wound in its body.

Stinger (X161). *Worker bees guard their hive from intruders, including robber bees and wasps that may attack and eat the larvae, honey, and even adult bees. The workers also sting people and animals that come too close to the hive.*

After the queen has mated, the workers may sting the males to death or push them out of the hive to die.

F

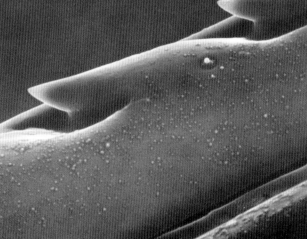

POLLEN

Flowering plants produce pollen, the male cells that carry half the genetic code needed to make new life. To create fruit and seeds, a grain of pollen from one flower must reach a pistil—the female part—of another flower. At the base of the pistil is the ovary, which contains the other half of the code.

Spruce and pine trees make a great deal of pollen. One pine cone may produce more than a *billion* grains. During spring and summer you may see pollen floating on a lake or coating a car parked under pine trees. It looks like yellow dust. Spruce and pine trees pollinate by means of the wind because they evolved 300 million years ago, before there were insects that pollinated plants.

Some more modern, flowering plants don't need wind—their pollen is carried around by insects and other animals. Bees are the most important pollinators, but other animals help, including butterflies, moths, wasps, ants, flies, birds, and bats.

Some plants can be pollinated by only one species of insect. The yucca, for example, lives across North America and relies on the yucca moth. The female yucca moth collects sticky yucca pollen and rolls it into a ball. She lays her eggs deep inside a yucca flower, then stuffs the pollen ball in after them, fertilizing the flower.

After emerging from their eggs, her larvae will eat some of the yucca seeds that result from this fertilization. Without yucca moths, yucca plants could not produce seeds and would die out. So would another kind of moth, *Prodoxus*, whose larvae feed only on yucca stems and seed pods.

Thanks to the SEM, scientists have been able to examine pollen more carefully than ever before. They have compared fossil pollen to today's pollen, for example, to learn about the past. By looking at pollen found near dinosaur bones, scientists have discovered what plants dinosaurs might have eaten.

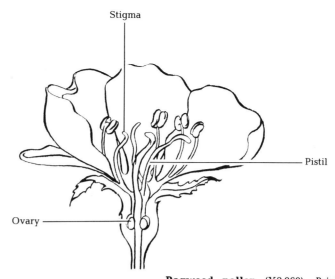

Ragweed pollen (X3,060). *Prickly pollen irritates some people's noses and makes them sneeze. It also sticks to insects better than smooth pollen, improving the chances that it will reach another flower.*

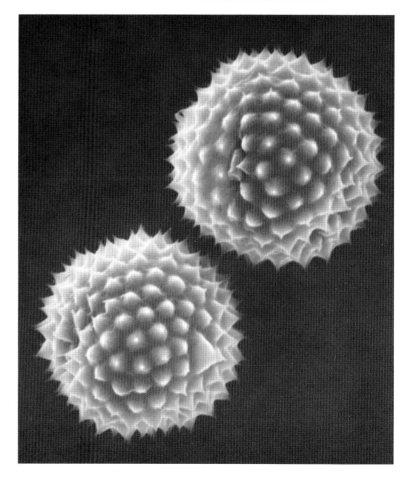

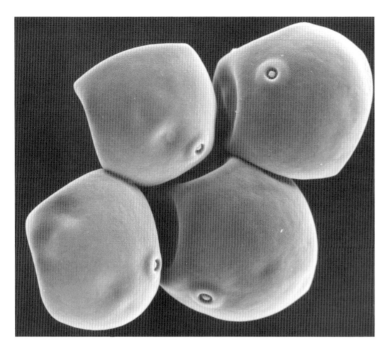

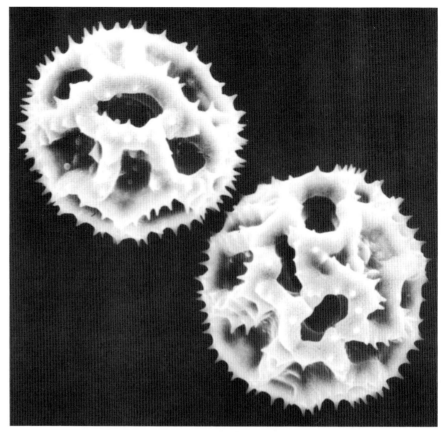

Corn pollen (X1,026). *Corn is a kind of grass that Native American farmers turned into a giant. When they found an especially large, healthy ear of corn, they used pollen from its tassels to fertilize other corn plants. The kernels, or seeds, produced by the hand-fertilized ears grew into slightly larger, healthier plants. In this way, Native American farmers carefully bred corn every year for thousands of years. Farmers today are still improving corn, by this and other methods.*

Dandelion pollen (X1,700). *Pollen is light and tough. Some has been found to travel more than a thousand miles on the wind, and last for years without losing its power to fertilize flowers.*

Dandelion seeds also fly on the wind, thanks to tiny hairs attached to each one, which forms a pappus, or parachute.

A grain of wild mustard pollen attached to stigma surface (X1,771). *A flower can make seeds only after it has been fertilized—after it has received the second half of the genetic code, which is contained in the pollen. As you see here, a tube may grow from the grain of pollen to one part of the stigma surface. The genetic code will pass through the tube to the ovary, giving the flower the ability to make a mustard seed.*

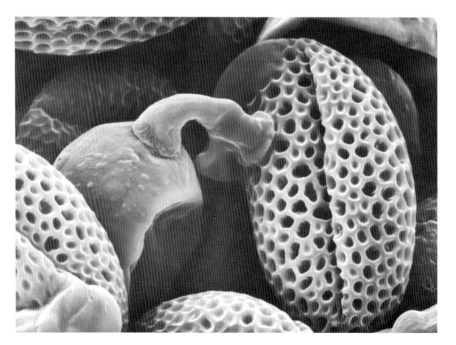

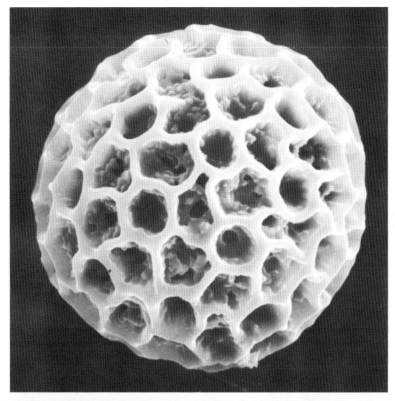

Pine pollen (X1,340). *Pine trees appeared before insects that pollinate trees and had to rely on wind to pollinate one another. To increase their chances of pollinating their neighbors, pine trees spend a lot of their energy making huge amounts of pollen.*

More modern plants rely on insects and other animals to deliver their pollen, which is a more accurate method of pollination. Modern plants thus save energy by making less pollen.

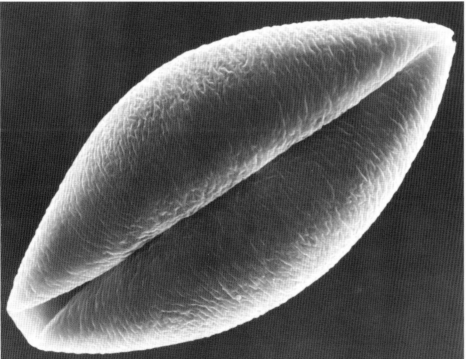

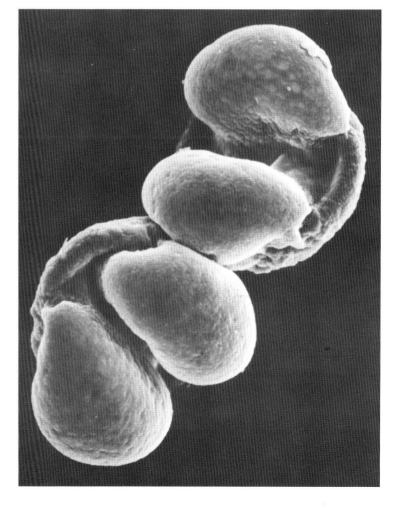

Cobea (X1,148) **and Tacca** (X2,565) **pollen.** *These two exotic kinds of pollen are carried from flower to flower by nectar-loving bats.*

Stomas of a pea leaf (X1,584). *Plants breathe through thousands of tiny "nostrils," called stomas, which can be opened and closed. They breathe carbon dioxide and exhale oxygen. Humans and other animals breathe oxygen and exhale carbon dioxide.*

Stoma of a horsetail leaf (X1,637). *Horsetail plants live all over the world in wet places. They have been around for a long time—horsetail fossils from the Carboniferous period, 345 to 290 million years ago (long before the dinosaurs), have been found.*

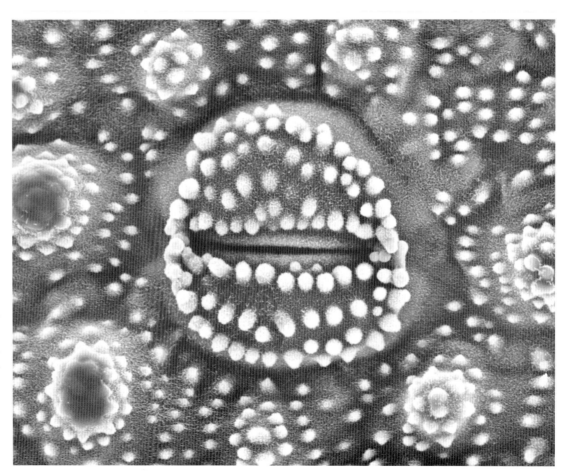

BUTTERFLY WINGS

Butterfly wings are clear. Their color comes from a covering of flat hairs, called scales.

The colors and designs of the scales do more than make beautiful patterns—they also help butterflies avoid being eaten. Some designs camouflage the insects and let them hide from hungry predators. Birds recognize other designs, such as the orange and black of the monarch butterfly, and stay away. Monarchs seem to taste terrible to birds.

Sulphur butterfly wing (X130). *The design on sulphur butterflies may help them recognize members of their own kind, or species, at mating time. They can't mate with a member of another species.*

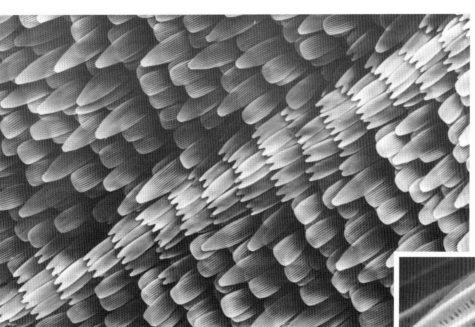

Single scale (X1,980). *Butterfly wing scales are strong and light—just right for flying. The scales have a thin coat of wax to make them waterproof.*

They can help a butterfly escape from a bird or spiderweb. The scales come off easily when the wings are touched, giving the insect a chance to slip away.

The scales are so light and fragile that they are hard to photograph in the SEM. A beam of electrons can knock them off the wing.

MOTHS

Like butterflies, most moths have long tongues and drink nectar from flowers. They are related, but most moths are nocturnal—they are active at night. The flowers they visit are often less colorful but better-smelling than flowers butterflies visit. In the dark, of course, sweet smells are more attractive than bright colors.

Most male moths have big furry-looking antennae to pick up the scent of females at mating time. Some moths' antennae are so sensitive they can detect a mate more than a mile away. Imagine if you could hear or smell another person at that distance!

The bodies of most moths are plump compared to those of butterflies. Some moths are bigger than small birds. The luna moth, for example, is one of the largest in North America. Its bright-green wings can span six inches from tip to tip.

Moth proboscis (X50). *This moth needs a long proboscis to reach deep into flowers. To keep it out of the way when not in use, the moth is able to curl it up.*

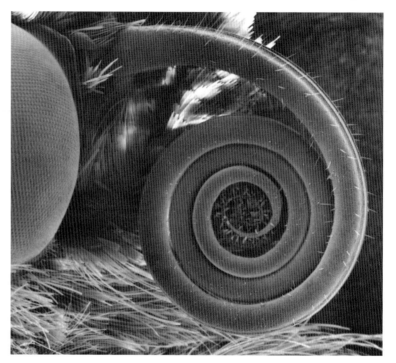

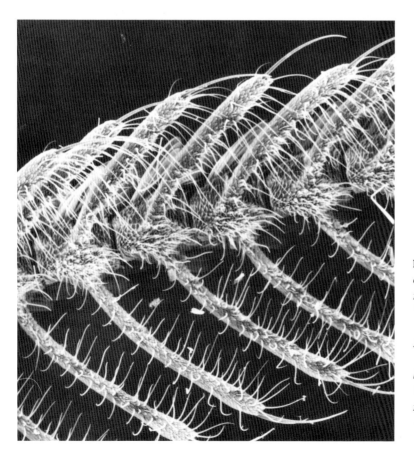

Moth antenna (X126). *This moth's large antenna is probably used to detect the scent of a mate, even one far away. The many hairs increase the chance that a tiny scent molecule will be caught and "smelled" by the moth.*

The moth could never see a mate at such a distance, even with its large eyes.

Some moths are able to hear the high-pitched squeaks of hunting bats and change direction—or stop flying and fall—to avoid them. These moths hear with tympana—thin, flexible areas on their bodies that vibrate in response to certain sounds.

BIRD FEATHERS

About 150 million years ago, animals similar to today's lizards began running on two legs. Over millions of years, their stiff scales changed, growing longer and softer, allowing the animals to glide between leaps.

Eventually, the scales evolved to become feathers. Over millions of years, gliding became flying and a new kind of animal emerged: the bird. Today there are about 9,000 *species* of birds, and more than 300 billion individual birds altogether.

Feathers not only allow birds to fly but also help them to keep cool in summer and warm in winter. Birds also use feathers to attract mates and shed water.

Different birds can dive at 180 miles an hour, hover, fly upside down and backward, and soar for days without landing. These aerobatics would be impossible without feathers.

Ruby-throated hummingbird feather (X130). *Feathers are light and have special shapes depending on how they're used. This hummingbird feather is small and narrow, like the hummingbird's wings, which beat in a figure-eight motion 53 times per second.*

The hummingbird's shimmering colors are not in the feathers but are caused by light scattering from the microscopic ridges on the feathers. You can see the colors only from certain angles—the hummingbird almost seems to sparkle as it moves.

This feather came from a hummingbird caught by Howard's cat, Harriet.

Ostrich feather (X112). *Hummingbirds are the smallest birds; ostriches are the largest. Ostriches can't fly—you can see how limp this feather is compared to the hummingbird's. But ostriches need their feathers to keep cool in the day and warm at night. They live in dry parts of Africa and Arabia, where there is little shade and the nights can be chilly.*

Ostriches also take dust baths, filling their feathers with fine dirt to discourage bloodsucking insects.

Great horned owl feather (X691). *This feather has been cut in half to show how it helps the owl hunt. The owl feather is bigger and softer than the stiff hummingbird feather, and it is hollow, making it especially quiet. Hummingbirds are noisy fliers— they "hum" like giant bugs. Owls must be silent to surprise the prey they swoop down on.*

Thick, hollow feathers create insulation by trapping air, so great horned owls stay warm in northern regions during the winter, when most hawks and other birds of prey have to go south.

MOSQUITOES

Female mosquitoes are one of the worst pests known to people and animals. As tiny and fragile as they are, mosquitoes sometimes spread disease. And even when mosquitoes don't make us sick, their bites make us itch.

Male mosquitoes are not bloodthirsty—they drink nectar from flowers and other plant juices, never blood. But most female mosquitoes need a meal of blood to produce eggs. They will bite birds, squirrels, deer, people, or almost any other animal.

Most female mosquitoes live only a few weeks, but after they get blood meals, each may lay as many as 200 eggs. Then, like vampires, they fly off to find someone else to bite.

As nasty as mosquitoes are to us, they provide food for many different kinds of animals, even the ones that get bitten, like birds. Fish, frogs, other insects, and spiders eat mosquitoes or mosquito larvae. Without mosquitoes, many animals would go hungry.

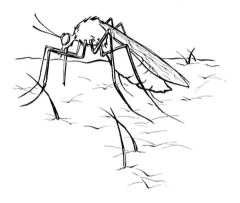

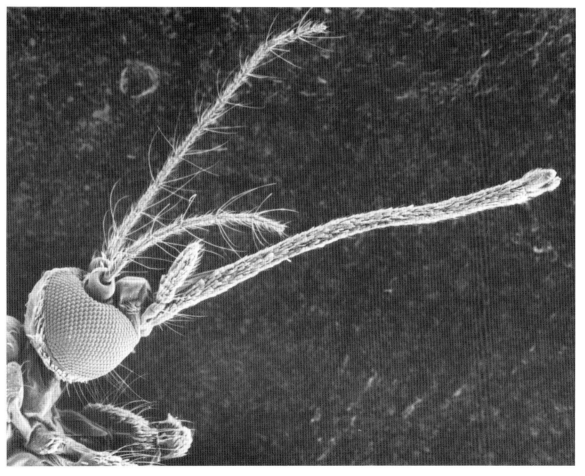

Female mosquito head (X56). *When a female mosquito lands on an animal, she lowers her mouth, or proboscis, to the skin.*

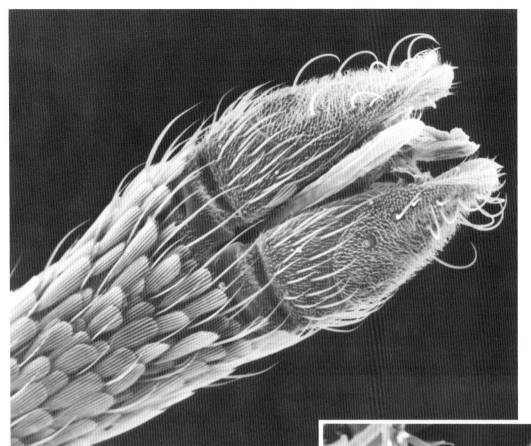

Proboscis end (X422). *After lowering her proboscis, the mosquito quickly slices into the skin and injects saliva into the wound. This makes blood flow freely—and also causes itching. The saliva may contain organisms that cause disease.*

In seconds, the microsurgery is complete. With the two halves of her feeding tube pressed together—you can see it here—the mosquito sucks up a meal of blood.

Proboscis tip (X3,248). *Inside the proboscis are four sharp blades—you can see two of them in this picture. They are so sharp you can barely feel them cut into your skin.*

Male mosquito head (X56). *The male mosquito, unlike the female, is a strict vegetarian. Instead of searching for animals to bite, he searches for female mosquitoes. The giant antennae help him find them.*

Male mosquito antenna (X311). *Scientists believe a male mosquito's antennae vibrate for only one sound: the beating of a female's wings.*

If a female is on his right, the right antenna will vibrate more, so the male will turn to the right. When both antennae are vibrating equally, he is heading straight for the female.

The portraits of the male and female are the same magnification (X56). It's easy to see how much larger the female is.

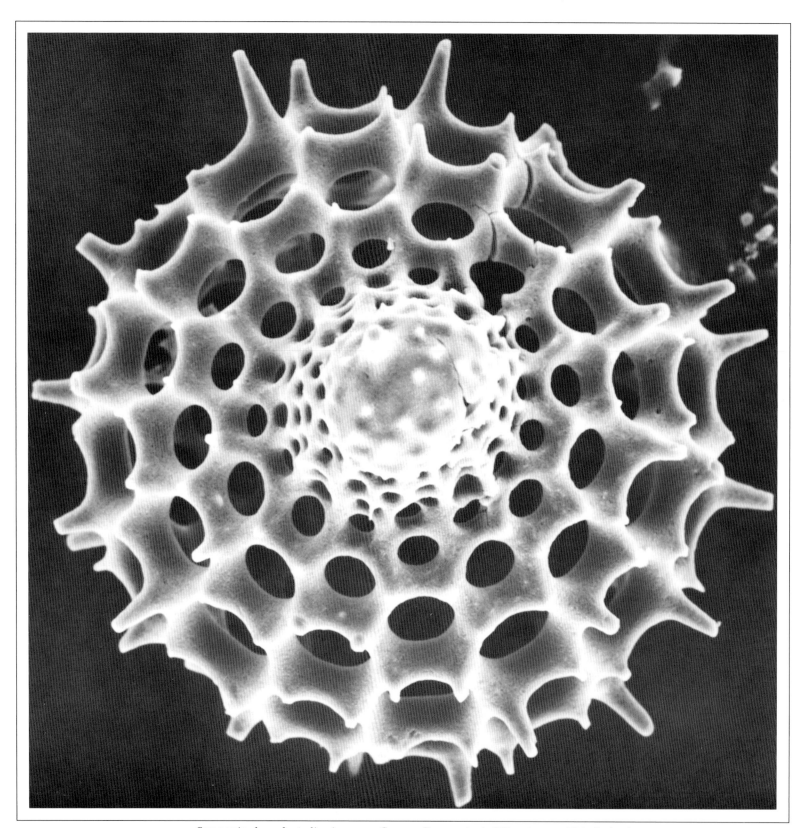

Some animals prefer to live in a cage. Can you figure out why? Turn to page 78 to find out.

WORLD TWO

The Water

The first life on our planet appeared in the water billions of years ago. No one knows how. All life on earth—including you and your family—is descended from those first microscopic living things. Most of the plants and animals on our planet still live in the water. Some have hardly changed.

SALT and SAND

Over millions of years, moving water in the sea and on land can wear down the biggest mountains and grind rocks and shells together until they are turned into pebbles, sand, and finally dust.

As streams and rivers carry water into the sea, they also carry minerals and salts from the land. As seawater evaporates to form clouds, the minerals are left behind. The seas get slightly saltier every year. Some, like Utah's Great Salt Lake, are so salty today that no fish can live in them.

Sand (X213). *You may have heard the saying "No two grains of sand are alike." Here are two very different grains Howard got in his shoe on a tropical island in the Indian Ocean. The piece above is a mineral; the tooth-shaped piece below is from a coral shell.*

These grains are especially small. The smaller the grains, the softer sand feels to the touch.

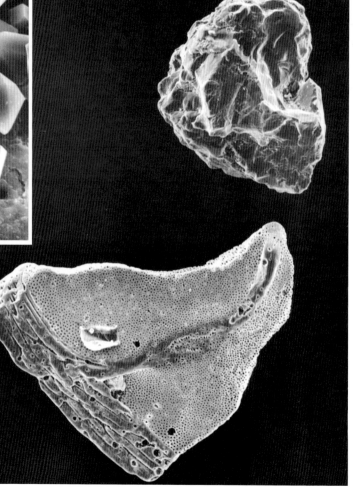

Sea salt on coral (X2,552). *All the water in lakes and rivers, and water from your tap, has some salt in it. Your body also contains salt—you can taste it in your tears, sweat, and blood. You need salt to complete certain chemical reactions in your body. Without salt, you couldn't survive.*

Seawater is much saltier than your body, and much too salty to drink. If you let seawater dry on your skin, salt crystals like these will form. As small as they are, you'll be able to feel and taste them.

ALGAE

Scientists think algae were the first things to live on our planet. An alga is a microorganism that, like a plant, gets energy from sunlight, but algae are much simpler than true plants.

All algae have only one cell, although some live together in groups. The largest algal organisms are seaweeds that can grow hundreds of feet long—longer than a blue whale, the largest animal.

In the hundreds of millions of years since algae first appeared, they have adapted to live almost anywhere. Some can live in polar ice, others in hot springs where no true plant or animal could survive. Some algae can survive in damp places on land, such as the shady sides of certain trees. In their long history, algae have even found a way to survive in places with little water: they join fungi to form lichen and live in some of the coldest, driest regions of the world, on mountaintops and near the South Pole.

Algae can be slimy and smelly, but some kinds make tasty salads. People aren't the only animals who eat it—algae is food for thousands of species.

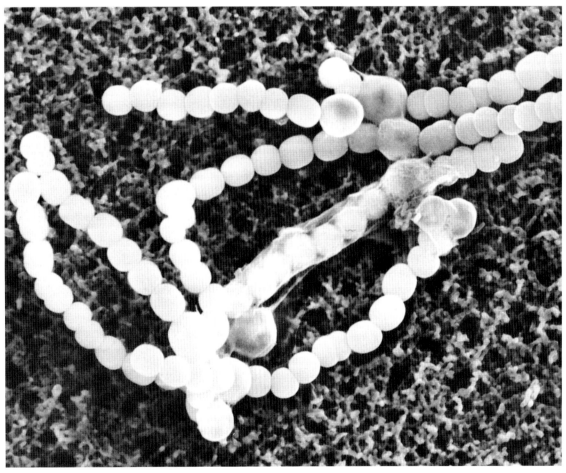

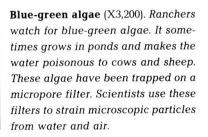

Blue-green algae (X3,200). *Ranchers watch for blue-green algae. It sometimes grows in ponds and makes the water poisonous to cows and sheep. These algae have been trapped on a micropore filter. Scientists use these filters to strain microscopic particles from water and air.*

27

DIATOMS AND OTHER MICROSCOPIC SKELETONS

Diatoms are algae that live all over the world, in ponds, streams, rivers, and oceans, as well as in damp soil and moss.

Diatoms get their energy from sunshine, like other plants, and are at the bottom of the food chain—many small animals eat them, and these animals are in turn eaten by larger animals.

Over millions of years, the tiny glass-like "skeletons" of dead diatoms have settled into layers on ocean and lake floors. These deposits are called diatomaceous earth, or diatomite. Filters made from this material can be used to purify water and other liquids. Dirt gets trapped in the tiny pores of the diatom skeletons, but the liquid passes through. Gardeners spread diatomite on the ground to stop invading snails—the diatom skeletons are too sharp for snails to crawl on. Diatomite is also used in toothpaste as a mild abrasive to scrape teeth clean.

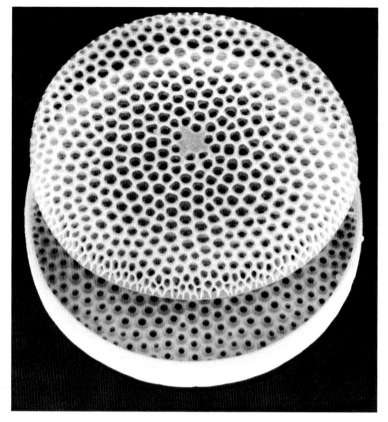

Centric diatom (X1,945). *This is the skeleton of a saltwater diatom.*

The cell walls fit together like a box and a lid, giving the alga shape and some protection from animals that would eat it. Holes in the walls help water and sunlight reach the inside of the cell.

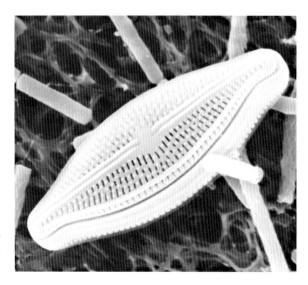

Pennate diatom (X5,500). *This diatom skeleton is surrounded by Bacillus bacteria on a micropore filter.*

Saltwater diatoms (X1,426). *Some diatoms can attach themselves to surfaces with a sticky jelly and slowly creep around. These are stuck to the surface of a seashell.*

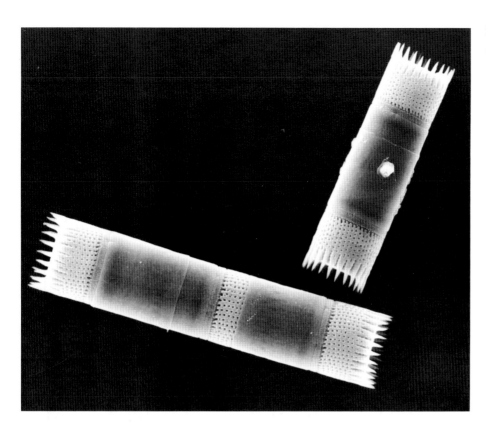

Freshwater diatoms (X1,782). *They may look like candy, but their skeleton is made of silica, a mineral.*

Foraminiferan shell (X370). *This is the skeleton of a one-celled animal that lived in the ocean. Foraminifera have been living, dying, and sinking to the ocean floor for many millions of years. As the shells pile up, they eventually turn into a chalky stone.*

The pyramids in Egypt are made from this stone—from billions and billions of foraminiferan shells.

Geologists use electron microscopes to examine foraminifera in rock. Because the animals have evolved steadily over millions of years—and died steadily in ever-deepening layers—the species of foraminifera in a rock can reveal how old it is.

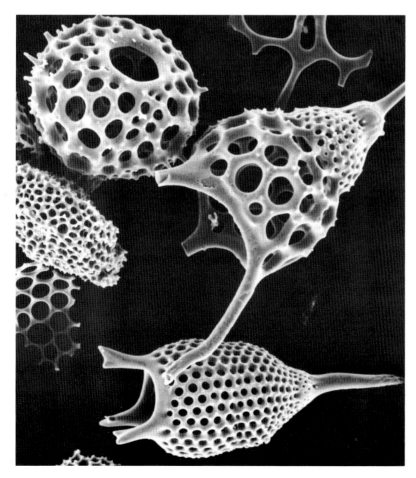

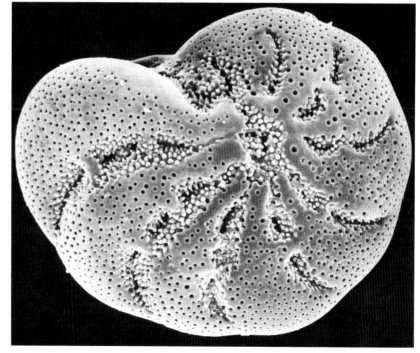

Radiolarian (X294). *A radiolarian is a one-celled animal that relies on a sharp, hard skeleton for protection. It reaches tiny arms through holes in its skeleton to grab particles of food.*

To keep from sinking, these animals carry droplets of oil inside their shells. The oil floats away after they die, and the skeletons sink to the bottom.

29

FISH

To be good swimmers, fish need to be smooth and slippery. Many human swimmers shave their entire bodies before a race so they will be as smooth as possible. Fast swimming can help fish win their races —and avoid getting eaten—but their skin can also work as camouflage and armor.

Some of a fish's enemies are microscopic, so its armor might include a slimy skin that prevents microscopic animals and bacteria from clinging to the fish. When a fish's skin is damaged—when you pick it up, for example—some of the slime may come off, making the fish more likely to get an infection.

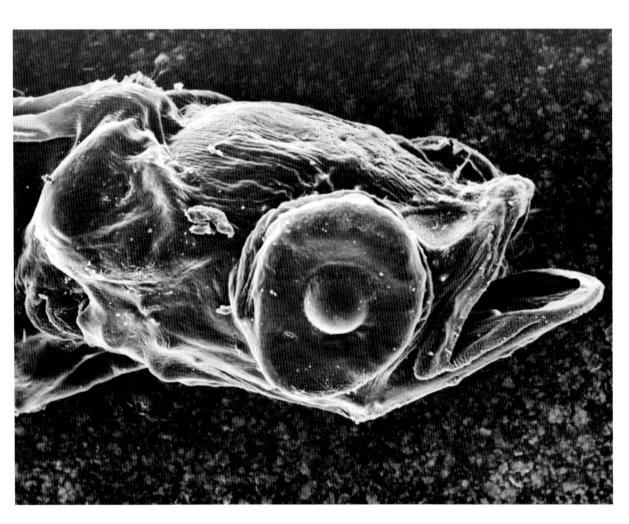

Herring larva (X143). *This immature fish has just broken out of its egg sac. It's much smaller than a minnow— and barely visible without a microscope. Fewer than one in a million larval fish grow to adulthood. The rest get eaten. That's why a herring lays many thousands of eggs at a time.*

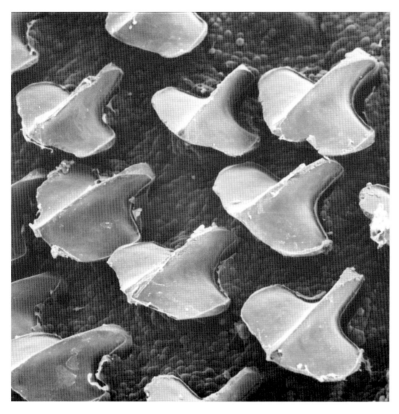

Rainbow trout scale (X176). *The microscopic ridges on trout scales reflect light so the fish looks iridescent, or shiny. This camouflages the fish—it seems to sparkle like the water and is very hard to see.*

The ridges also help hold the film of slime called mucilage that helps a trout move easily through the water and protects it from parasites.

Shark skin (X167). *Shark skin is so rough that samurai warriors used it to cover their sword handles—it gave fighters a good grip even when their hands were bloody.*

A shark's skin is rough because "teeth" grow from it. Dermal denticles are made of the same material as the shark's teeth.

No one knows for sure why sharks have such rough skin. It may make them less appetizing to other fish, or it may make water flow over their skin better. Dermal denticles point toward the shark's tail.

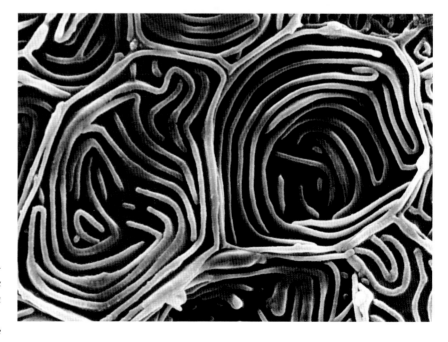

Goldfish skin (X5,946). *Goldfish have a thin skin covering their scales. Like the trout scale, the microscopic patterns on the skin make it shiny and help it hold a thin layer of mucilage.*

Goldfish have been kept as pets for centuries. The most colorful fish have been selected and allowed to mate so that goldfish today have brilliant colors.

WATER BEETLES, STRIDERS, AND WHIRLIGIGS

Water beetles, striders, and whirligigs live in the world where air and water meet. They are predators —they eat other animals.

You'll find water beetles hunting animals much larger than themselves in ponds and quiet streams around the world. The water beetle is fierce both as a larva and as an adult. You might get pinched if you try to catch one.

Water striders and whirligigs are so small and light they can walk on water. They're constantly moving to avoid birds, frogs, and other hungry animals.

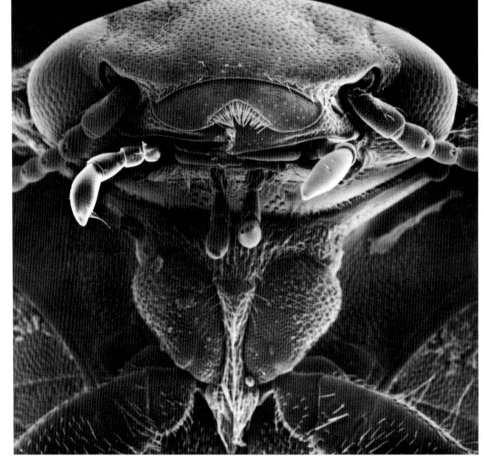

Diving beetle (X120). *This is one of the predaceous insects that swim underwater. It eats snails, tadpoles, and even small fish.*

Water beetles will sometimes float head down in the water, watching for prey. When they spot victims, they dive, carrying their air supply in bubbles under their elytra— their outer wings—or trapped in their body hairs.

Diving beetle rear leg (X46). *All diving beetles have to be fast swimmers. Special rows of hairs turn their rear legs into paddles to help the beetles shoot through the water.*

Not only are they good swimmers and divers—most water beetles can also fly.

Whirligig (X46). *Whirligig beetles, like many predators, are also prey. As they skim over the surface of the water, whirligigs have to look for food below them and birds or other predators above. They have four eyes—two smaller eyes look up to the sky and two larger eyes look down into the water. You can see one of each in this picture.*

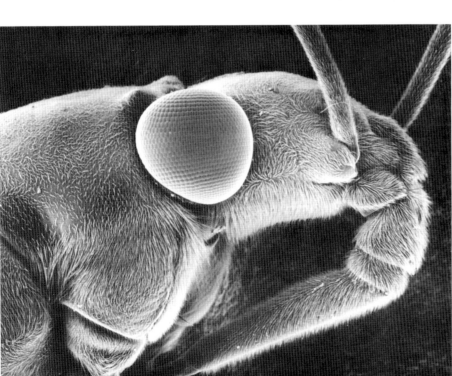

Water strider (X41). *Water striders are covered with special hairs that repel water so they can "stand" on calm water without getting wet.*

They stand on four legs and use the front pair for grabbing other insects to eat.

Their eyesight is good—they will notice you if you move. Just try to catch one.

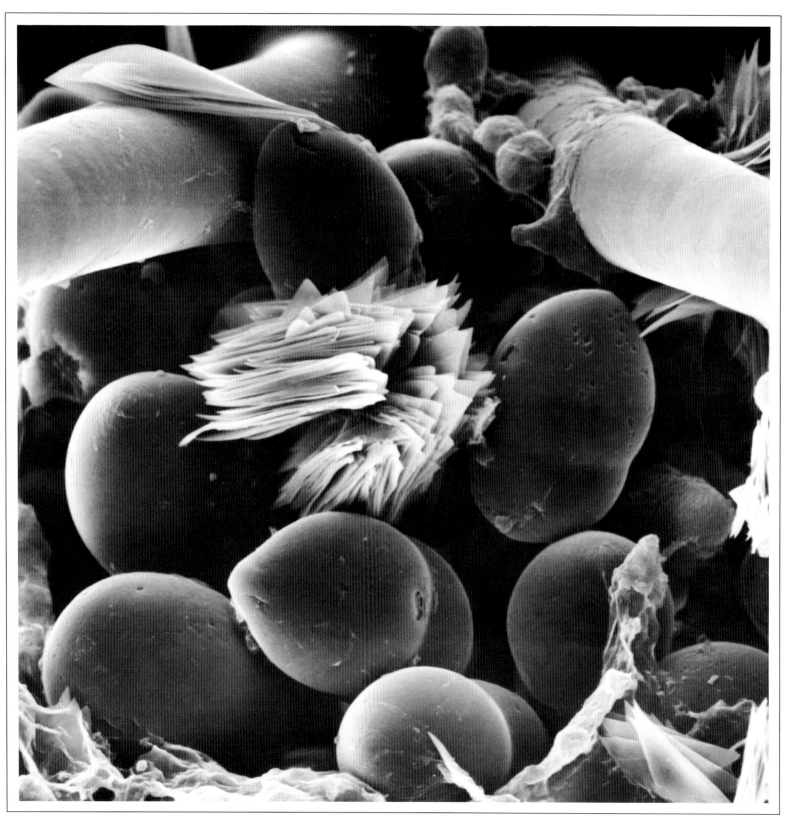

The animal that deposited these eggs left behind something to protect them. Can you spot it? Turn to page 78 to find out more.

WORLD THREE

The Yard

To most of the animals in your back yard, you're a giant. To some of them, your toes would seem as big as houses. But as small as their world is, it is so complicated and dangerous that most are too busy to notice an enormous MacroAlien like you.

ANTS, APHIDS, and LADYBUGS

In the game of life, ants are winners—there are more ants than any other land animal. For every hundred pounds of human being there are two or three *thousand* pounds of ants.

Most insects have short lives, but worker ants may live for several years. Queens may live to be fifteen years old.

Ants live from the cold arctic to the hot tropics. For their size, they are some of the fiercest animals known.

Like worker bees, all worker ants are sisters, children of the queen. Males don't work—they live only to mate. A queen ant mates only once. She stores sperm from males inside her body for the rest of her life. Each sperm contains half the genetic code the queen needs to fertilize an egg and create new female ants. (Male ants are produced from non-fertilized eggs.)

When an ant colony reaches a certain population, or at a certain time of year, new queens will be born in the colony. They must leave the nest and establish new colonies of their own. Some mate and fly off alone. Others take some workers and walk.

When a queen finds a new nesting place, she tears off her wings, if she has any, and begins to lay eggs that will become new workers. The queen will never fly again. Workers will bring her food and tend to her needs.

Ants lead complex lives. Allegheny mound ants steal the pupae, or undeveloped ants, of another species and raise them as slaves. Other ants grow tiny mushrooms in their nest for food.

Some ants "herd" aphids and drink their honeydew, a sweet excretion. Like cowboys, these ants move their aphids around to plants that are good aphid food. One kind of ant in Argentina even builds tiny shelters, like barns, to protect its aphids.

In the microworld of ants and aphids, ladybugs are the wolves. Ladybugs eat aphids, so ants try to kill ladybugs. Ladybugs bite back, but they also have a more unusual weapon: they squeeze their own blood out between their leg joints. The blood is sticky and can gum up an ant's attack.

Worker ant (X37). *This ant doesn't have as many facets, or lenses, in her eye as other insects we've looked at. Most worker ants can't see very well—they find their way around by touching and smelling with their antennae.*

This ant also has ocelli, simple eyes. You can see one ocellus in the middle of this ant's forehead. The ocellus has only one lens. It probably isn't good for seeing movement, but it may be able to detect light intensity.

Claw (X246). *Ants are strong; some can carry as much as fifty times their own weight. That would be like a full-grown man carrying a five-ton school bus.*

The pouch in the center of the claw is a suction cup the ant can use to cling to smooth surfaces like leaves.

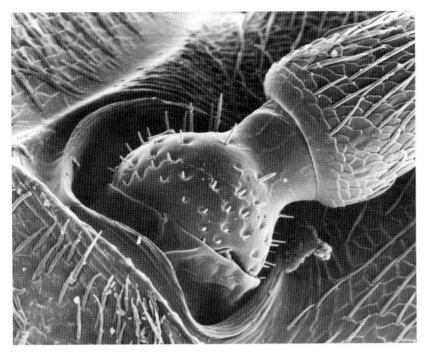

Base of ant antenna (X506). *Ants can't feel much through their hard shell, or exoskeleton, but they have sensitive antennae to help them find their way, even in the total darkness of a nest. The antennae can feel and smell.*

They can move their antennae around thanks to the kind of ball-and-socket joint you see in this picture. A tiny piece of dust is stuck to the right side of the socket.

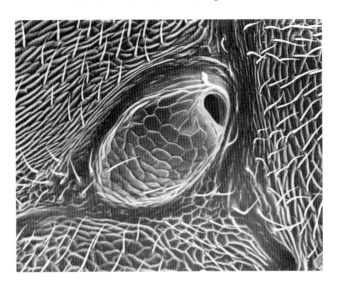

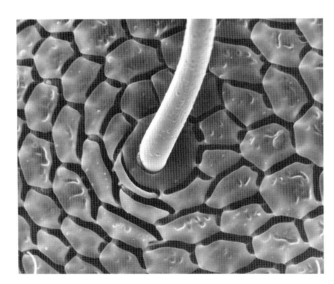

Cuticle and seta (X1,426). *An ant's shell is like armor. The hair that grows from the skin, or cuticle, may be attached to a nerve under the cuticle to help the ant feel its surroundings.*

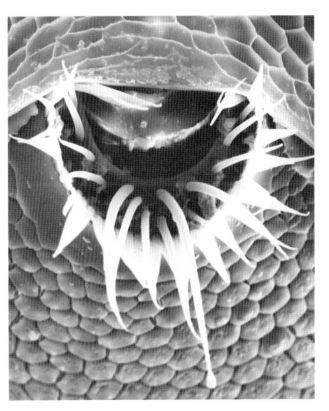

Ant anus (X902). *Like all living things, ants create waste inside their bodies and need to get rid of it. This is where an ant expels its tiny crystal feces, which make excellent fertilizer for plants.*

Some ants can shoot acids from this opening as a defense.

37

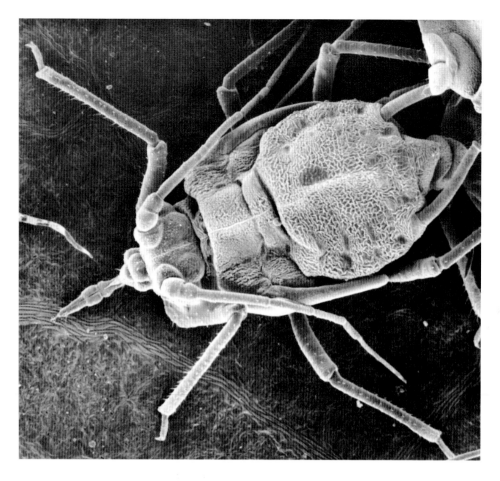

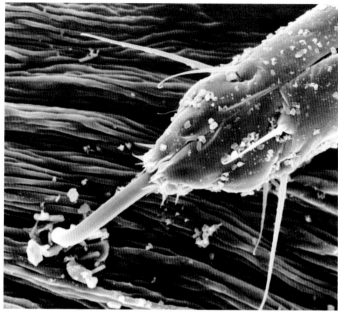

Aphid (X68) **and proboscis** (X1,049). *Human gardeners think aphids are pests—this one is sucking the juices out of a bean leaf.*

Aphids can be killed with poison, but some gardeners buy ladybugs instead. Ladybugs, turned loose in the garden, eat aphids by the thousands—no poison required.

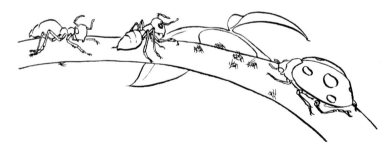

Aphid cornicles (X259). *Aphids have one defense against ladybugs and their other enemies: glue. When attacked, they squirt a sticky cement from their cornicles, the two tubes in this picture. It will make a ladybug's claws stick to the leaf and gum up its wings if it doesn't fly away.*

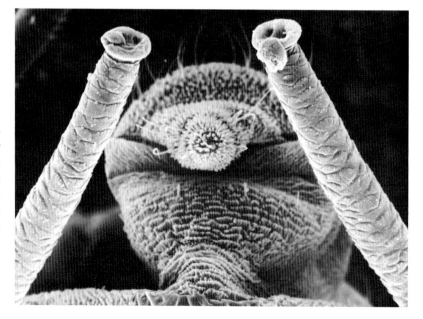

Ladybug head (X115). *Ladybugs may look cute to us, but their jaws are big enough to kill an aphid with a single bite. The mouth parts, made for chewing, identify the ladybug as a beetle, not a true bug.*

As fierce as the ladybug is, it can kill only a few aphids before the squirts of glue and other chemicals alert nearby aphids that they are under attack and should begin squirting their own glue.

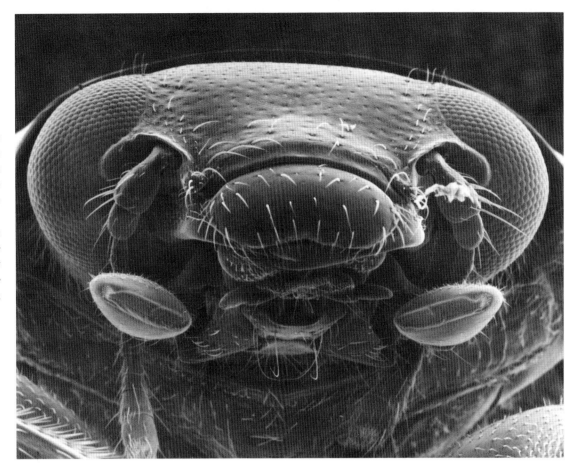

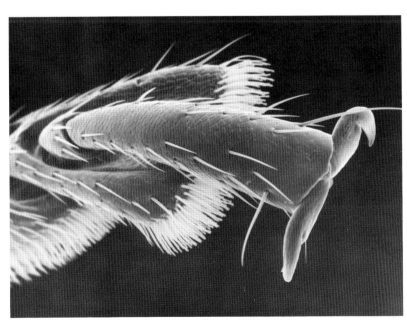

Ladybug claw (X207). *The thick setae on the underside of its front legs may help this kind of ladybug grab prey or a mate in a tiny bear hug. The flexible hairs may give the legs a better grip than hard, bare exoskeleton would.*

MOLDS

True molds are a kind of fungus. They have no chlorophyll—they can't use sunlight the way plants do—so they have to get their energy from living things, as parasites, or by consuming dead things.

Molds send out rootlike threads into soil, fruit, bread, or other moist things they can use as food. The threads absorb nutrients and grow. Eventually you can see and smell them.

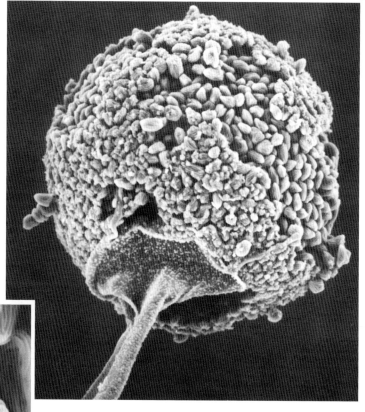

Mold fruiting structure (X644) **and spores** (X3,696). *After the rootlike mold cells grow together, they produce spores, their primitive seeds. The spores will spread out, and if the environment is damp and warm enough, they'll form new mold colonies.*

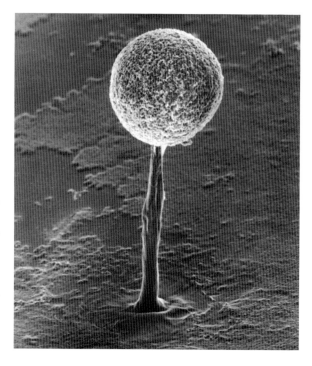

Slime mold fruiting body (X125). *You'll find slime molds on logs in the woods. They usually look like yellow or orange jelly.*

At first, scientists thought they were true molds, and slime molds do behave like molds in some ways, but this kind of slime mold, Lamproderma, is not related to fungi.

Lamproderma spores send chemical signals to each other when it's time to produce more spores. Then they crawl together, almost like single-celled animals, to form a fruiting body like this one. When the new spores are made, they are released into the air and the cells of the fruiting body go their separate ways.

SPIDERS

All spiders have eight legs, and most have eight eyes. They're related to other eight-legged animals like ticks, scorpions, and daddy longlegs.

Every spider makes silk, though not all make webs. Liquid silk is produced by special glands inside a spider's body. It hardens when the spider draws it from the glands through its spigots, which extend from fingerlike projections called spinnerets. Most spiders have six spinnerets.

Silk is much stronger and more flexible than steel would be if it were drawn so thin. Spiders make eight different kinds of silk—some spiders can make more than one. They use some to make webs, a different kind to wrap paralyzed victims, and another to wrap eggs.

Baby spiders and some small adults use a special silk to make "parachutes." When the wind blows, the spiders catch it in their silky sails and take off into the air on a one-way trip, destination unknown.

Some different kinds of spiders are so similar—and so small—that an arachnologist, a spider expert, may need an SEM to tell them apart. Every species of spider has different reproductive organs, which may be too small to examine without an electron microscope.

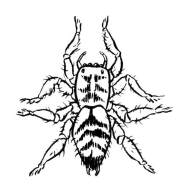

Jumping spider head (X55). The two eyes on the top of the head probably have a different focal length from the others. The upper eyes may see things at a distance, such as a bird looking for a spider. The bigger eyes can be focused and may see things close up, such as an insect the spider can eat.

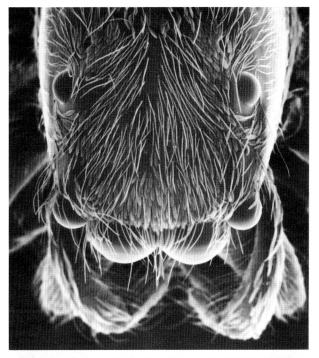

Jumping spider setae (X543). *Some spiders are furry, but they don't have soft skin—they have a hard exoskeleton. To feel wind and things they touch, they have special hairs—trichobothria—attached to joints and nerves under their exoskeletons. The trichobothrium in the lower right corner has a joint in a socket.*

The other hairs, called setae, don't have any feeling—they just give the spider color.

Jumping spider head (X67). *The jumping spider needs to see well because it doesn't spin a web or wait for prey—it jumps onto its victims and bites them. That may be why it has such large eyes compared to the size of its body.*

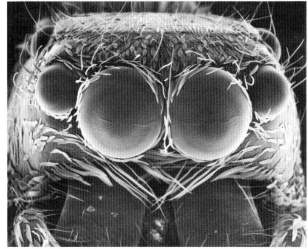

41

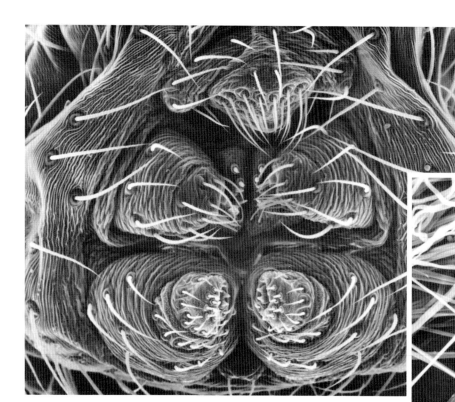

Spiderweb (X2,059). *Look closely at a steel cable holding up a bridge and you'll see it is made of many wires twisted together, not a single strand. As you can see in this picture, spider silk doesn't come out in a single strand, either. If one strand breaks, others can take up the slack.*

Hammock spider spinnerets (X377). *Some spiders make huge webs to catch prey, while others use silk only to wrap their eggs, protecting them from weather and predators.*

This spider gets its name from the large sheet webs it builds to snare its victims.

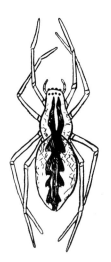

Hammock spider tarsus (X827). *Most spiders catch live prey and bite it, injecting venom. Spiders need special feet, or tarsi, to hold prey and to walk on and manipulate their webs.*

These tarsi seem delicate, but they, along with the legs, can hold struggling insects, even those larger than the spider, until they are paralyzed by the spider's venom.

Praying mantis head (X71). *The praying mantis probably sees well— it has large compound eyes and hunts for food soon after it comes out of its egg case. Each facet of its eye can see a single image at a time, like one of the tiny dots on your TV screen. Eyes like these are especially good for spotting movement— the movement of enemies like birds and the movement of prey like flies.*

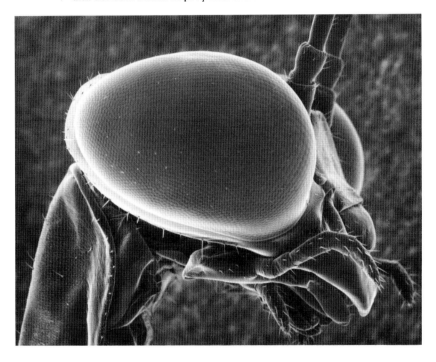

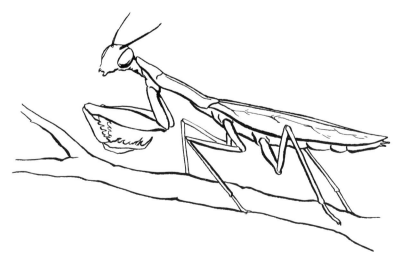

PRAYING MANTISES

Praying mantises are related to roaches, but instead of eating dead things, as roaches do, mantises are predators. Human gardeners like praying mantises because they eat aphids and other pests. Praying mantises, like ladybugs, can be bought through the mail and let loose in the garden.

Female mantises sometimes eat more than garden pests—they have been known to eat their mates. By contributing his body as a big meal during or after mating, the male mantis may give the female a better chance to survive and lay the eggs he has fertilized.

Mantis jaws (X111). *These sharp jaws, known as mandibles, can kill another insect in a flash. They are serrated like steak knives to cut more effectively.*

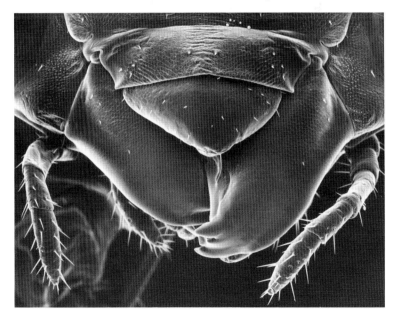

PLANTS

We animals could not have lived on earth before plants and other photosynthetic organisms had been here a long time. They were around for hundreds of millions of years before us, before dinosaurs and even before insects. Plants inhale carbon dioxide and exhale oxygen. When the earth was formed, the atmosphere had so much carbon dioxide that it would have been poisonous for animals to breathe. After breathing carbon dioxide for hundreds of millions of years, plants created enough oxygen for insects, dinosaurs, and animals like us.

Individual plants can grow and reach out with branches and roots, but they can't really move from place to place. Instead, they send seeds through the air and across the water to colonize new areas. Some plants rely on animals to carry their seeds to new ground.

In many places, plants must fight for sunlight, water, and minerals in the soil. By spreading leaves and blocking out the light, they prevent new plants from taking root.

Plants may seem peaceful, but they must struggle to survive. Some plants even release poison when they are attacked by insects.

Wild mustard flower petal (X1,720). *Flowers are designed to attract pollinators, most of which are insects. All flowers offer a reward to the animals that pollinate them, usually tasty pollen or sweet nectar. Some flowers smell good, others have beautiful colors and designs. Flowers from the mustard plant are bright yellow.*

Grapevine tendril (X120). *To reach the sun, grapevines climb up and over other plants or anything else that stands still. The hairs on this tendril may help it cling to rough surfaces to continue its climb.*

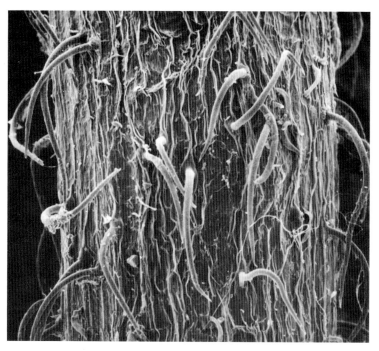

Seed pod (X174). *The hooks on this burdock seed pod attach to passing animals, including people, who unknowingly spread the seeds far and wide.*

Velcro (X29). *Velcro is a machine-made fiber based on the design of the seed-pod surface. The hooks you see in this picture attach to tiny loops on its sister fabric.*

Georges de Mestral, a Swiss scientist, found seed pods sticking to his clothes after a walk he took in 1948. Looking at the seeds under a microscope, he saw tiny hooks. De Mestral spent the next eight years figuring out how to make Velcro.

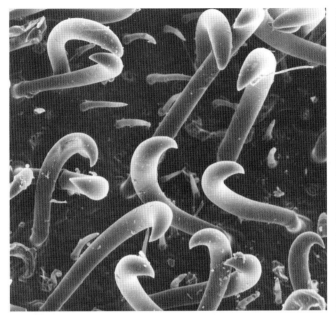

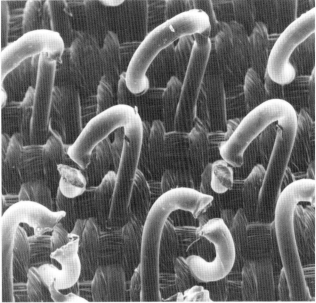

Oak wood (X131). *This cross section of oak shows the stiff cell walls packed together. This design makes the wood stiff enough to stand, yet flexible enough to bend in the wind.*

People have imitated this design to make cardboard. Look at the edge of a piece of cardboard and see for yourself.

Vein in mahogany wood (X285). *Like all living things, plants pass fluids through their bodies. Minerals and water, mixed together, flowed through this vein in a mahogany tree.*

The tree has been cut down, but the vein stays open because the walls of a tree's cells are stiff—much stiffer than an animal's cell walls. That's how a tree can stand up without bones or muscles.

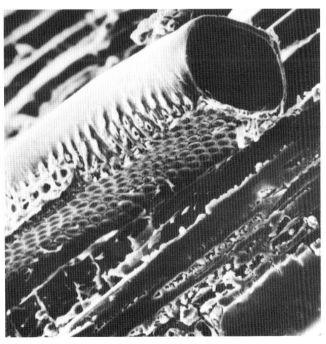

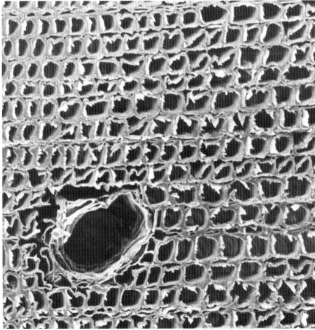

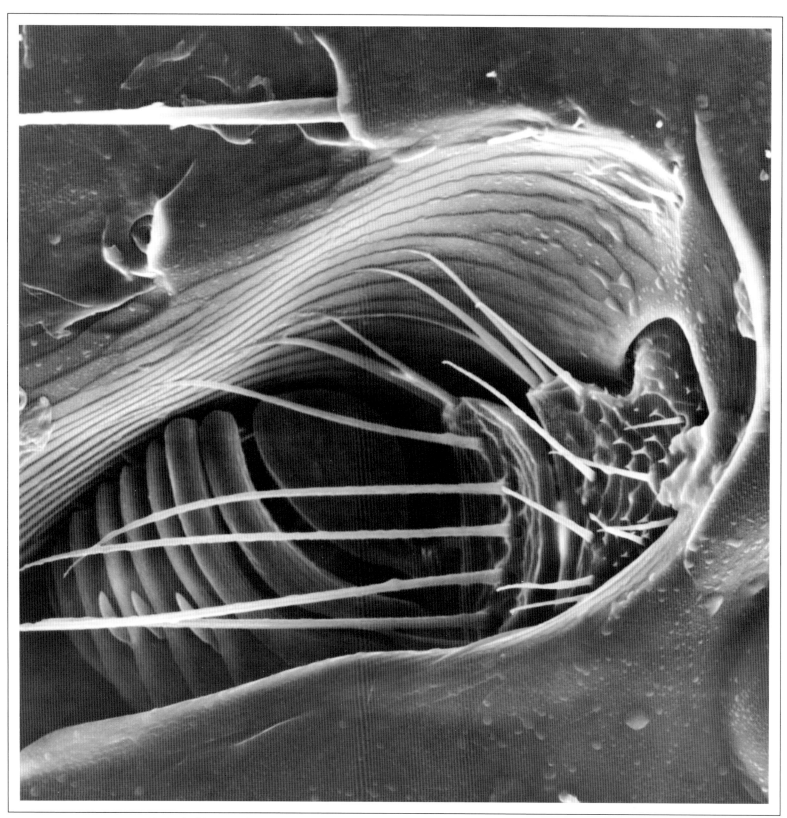

You're looking into the ear of an animal that could fit into your ear. Turn to page 79 to find out more.

WORLD FOUR

The Home

A house is a wonderful place to live. If it's well built, it stays warm in the winter, cool in the summer, and dry all year round—although there are a few places that are almost always wet. There are also good things to eat, soft places to sleep, and dark places to hide. No wonder so many living things want to share our homes with us.

HOUSEHOLD FUNGI

Fungi are some of the weirdest, smelliest, most helpful living things on earth. Unlike algae and other plants, fungi can't get energy from sunlight. And unlike bacteria, most fungi can't swim or crawl. But like algae and bacteria, fungi are a key part of life on earth.

When a tree falls, for example, its water and nutrients are locked inside the hard, dry wood. A fungus can break down the wood and "unlock" the water and food inside for its own use—and for other plants and animals. Raccoons, for instance, can't eat wood, but they do eat mushrooms—fungi—that grow on logs. When fungi have broken down a log enough, raccoons may make a home in the hollow inside. After fungi have softened the log even more, plants take root in it, using the dead tree's nutrients for their own growth.

Other kinds of fungi give babies diaper rash and people athlete's foot. Fungus can grow in your sneakers and make them smell bad.

Yeast, another fungus, makes bread rise as the yeast cells consume sugar and expel carbon dioxide. Without yeast, bread would be dense and hard, not light and soft.

Sealed in a bottle of grape juice, yeasts can also consume sugar and excrete alcohol until the alcohol gets too strong and kills them. Their dead bodies can sometimes be seen in clumps at the bottom of a bottle of red wine.

A huge fungus in the state of Washington was discovered recently by mycologists, mushroom experts. As big as 400 city blocks, it is much larger and heavier than any animal that has ever lived on earth, even the biggest dinosaur. It lives underground—people notice it only when mushrooms grow up out of it and sprout on the ground or on trees. This mighty fungus may be more than a thousand years old. Bigger, older fungi are sure to be lurking underground somewhere else—they just haven't been discovered yet.

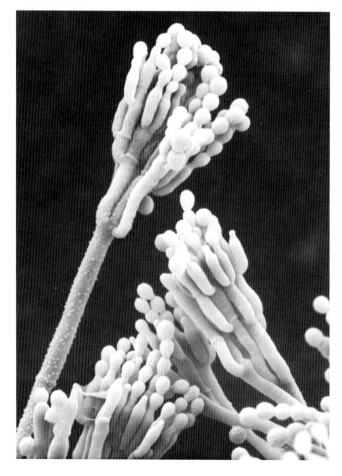

Penicillium (X1,610). *This pale bread mold stops infections in people by preventing the formation of cell walls in new bacteria cells. Before scientists discovered how to make the drug penicillin from this mold, people often died from wounds that became infected with bacteria. Penicillin now saves thousands of people's lives every year.*

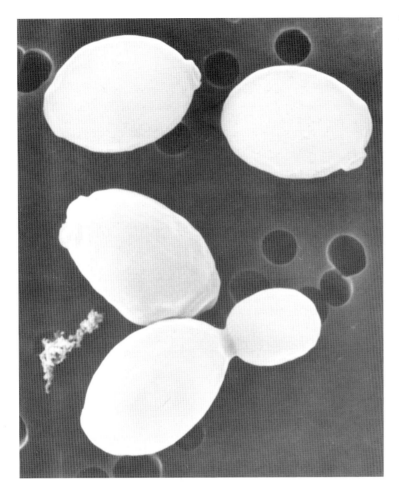

Wine yeast (X9,832). *These fungal microorganisms eat sugar and excrete alcohol, their form of waste.*

The yeast on the bottom is making a copy of itself by budding, or dividing in two. Budding leaves a "scar"—you can see two bud scars on the upper yeast.

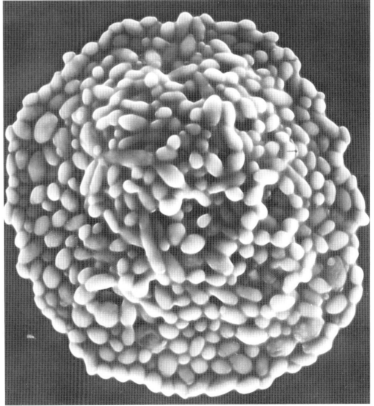

Colony of Saccharomyces (X1,399). *These fungi are mixed into dough with sugar. As they consume the sugar, they expel gas bubbles to make spaces in the dough for a light, airy bread.*

Yeast are easy to kill—if they are too warm or cold, they die and the bread won't rise. In any event, they are all killed when the bread is baked.

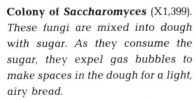

BACTERIA

Bacteria were among the first creatures on earth. They are small—one drop of water may contain *hundreds of millions* of them. They live almost everywhere: in water, soil, and the bodies of other organisms. Billions of bacteria live on you and inside you. Bacteria even live in the air.

Some of the bacteria in and on our bodies help us fight off other bacteria that would hurt us.

When you get a cut, washing it with soap and water makes your skin slippery—most of the harmful bacteria slide off. Your body's defenses will usually kill the few still on the cut, preventing an infection.

Cows have bacteria inside them to digest the grass they eat. Some termites have bacteria in their guts to digest wood.

Many plants need bacteria in the soil to survive. The bacteria take nitrogen gas out of the air and change it to nitrates plants can use.

Some deep-water fish use blobs of glowing bacteria to light up the darkness of their world.

Bacteria are a key part of life on earth, but we need to keep them in balance. Having too many bacteria inside us is as bad as having too few.

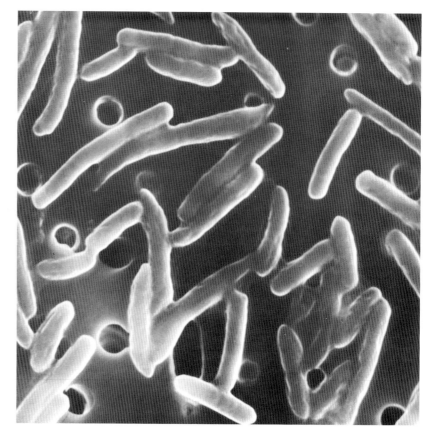

Escheriscia coli (X8,107). E. coli *is one of the world's most common bacteria. Millions of them live in the intestines of mammals, including you. The bacteria help break down the food you eat into molecules your body can use.*

E. coli *might cause an infection if you got them in your mouth or in a cut.*

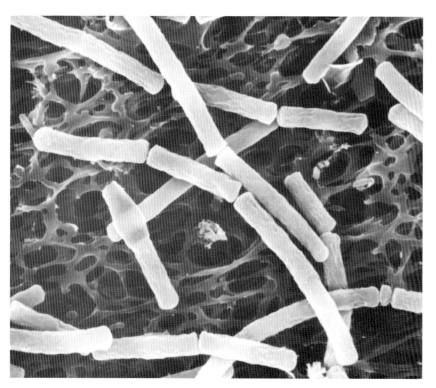

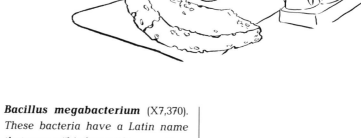

Bacillus megabacterium (X7,370). *These bacteria have a Latin name that means "big beast," because they are so large compared to other bacteria. They live in soil. Scientists can use them as living factories because they excrete valuable chemicals.*

Mildew and bacteria on a kitchen sponge (X1,091). *Sponges help in the kitchen because their pores soak up soap, water, and dirt. Most of the stuff you scrub off your dishes goes down the drain, but some of it stays in the pores of the sponge.*

Bacteria and fungi live everywhere. With the right amounts of water, air, and food, they will grow. Eventually, you can see and smell them.

The bacteria in this picture look like blobs; the fungi look like threads. The background is a sponge from Dennis's kitchen.

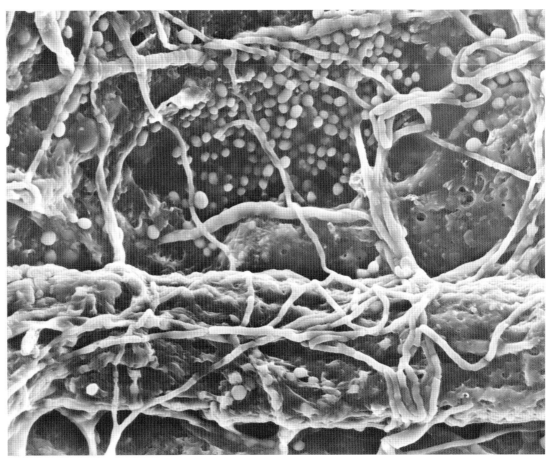

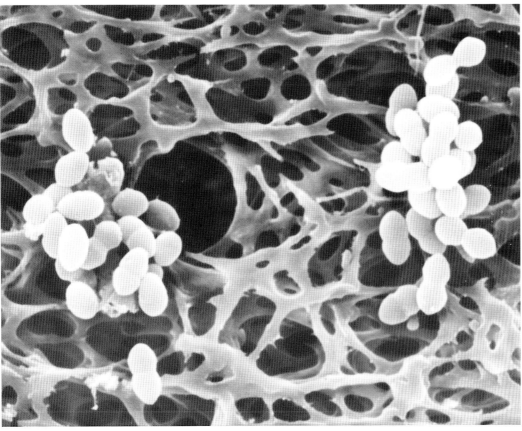

Streptococcus (X12,420). *These are colonies of bacteria that group together in chains and can cause strep infections in people. The colony on the left is clinging to a blob of slime it produced. In the background is a micropore filter.*

When Dennis works with dangerous bacteria like Streptococcus, he wears rubber gloves and a surgical mask, and works with his hands under a big glass box so he can see what he's doing but won't get splashed with bacteria. When he's finished, he washes carefully.

MITES

You probably have mites right under your nose—they live on the hairs on your upper lip. Most people also have mites on their eyelashes and in their ears. Mites live almost everywhere, from mountaintops to ocean depths. There may be up to a million different kinds, but only about 50,000 have been described by scientists.

Like algae, some mites survive frozen in ice. Others live in hot springs at 120 degrees Fahrenheit. Like spiders and scorpions, their relatives, adult mites have eight legs. (When they're born, mites have only six legs.)

One species of mite spends its whole life in a moth's ear. Others live in the lungs of dogs, monkeys, seals, birds, and snakes. Some even live on fleas—that's how tiny they are.

In bright light, you might see a dust mite if it was alone on a sheet of black paper. (Dust mites are cream-colored, and more than a dozen would fit on the period at the end of this sentence.) But it couldn't see you. Mites are blind.

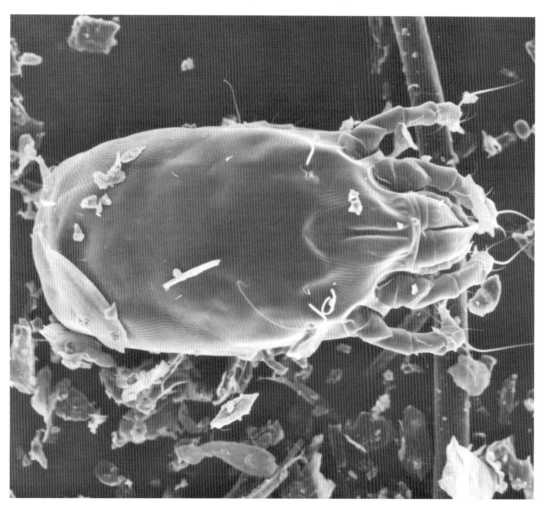

Dust mite (X391). *There are about fifteen kinds of dust mites. Some of them live in your bed, eating the millions of dead skin cells that fall off your body every hour. They also live in dust balls behind your bed and around the house.*

This mite is clinging to a machine-made fiber. You can see a featherlike insect scale on its back. The scale may have fallen off a moth's wing.

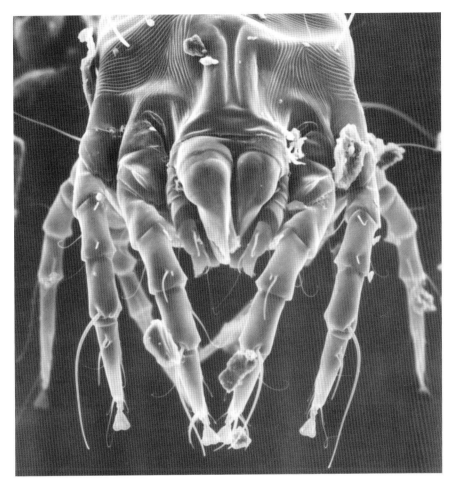

Dust mite (X598). *Mites won't hurt you on purpose, but they might make you sneeze. Everybody inhales a few mites now and then, and some people are allergic to them.*

But many people are allergic to mite excrement. Mites concentrate the allergin—the stuff that makes us sneeze—in their fecal packets. These "packets" are so small and light they float in the air. They can get into our nose, making us sneeze.

Mites are small but tough. Their skin is like armor. Go ahead and vacuum them—no place could be more perfect for dust mites than a vacuum bag full of dust.

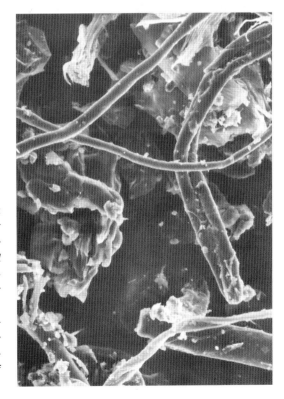

House dust (X419). *The dust in your house is partly you—your dead skin cells and hair. You can see many different kinds of things in this sample of dust. The smooth fibers are machine-made. The rougher, twisted fiber in the bottom corner looks like cotton. In the background, in the upper right corner, you can see what may be insect parts.*

Police investigators sometimes use an SEM to compare fibers and hairs found at a crime scene with those found on suspected criminals. If the fibers match perfectly, it's possible that the suspect was at the scene of the crime.

FIBERS

The various fibers we use feel different to the touch and have different uses. Cotton feels better than nylon next to your skin, for example, but nylon is stronger and can be woven more tightly to repel water.

By looking at fibers under the SEM, we can tell something about how they were made and what they might be good for.

Cotton (X58). *Cotton makes good towels and T-shirts because its thick, soft fibers soak up moisture and hold it like a sponge. Cotton feels cool because it holds moisture next to your skin.*

Each cotton fiber is the outer edge of a cell that was attached to the seed of a cotton plant. The fibers can grow up to two inches long.

Woven sheep hair (X73). *Wool makes good yarn because the long and curly hairs are covered with lanolin, an oily substance that helps the hairs cling together. Wool keeps you warm because the thick fibers trap air and create insulation. Also, the fibers "wick" moisture away from your body, making wool feel dry to the touch.*

As you can see in this picture, each wool thread is made of many hairs twisted together.

Nylon (X58). *You would not want to use nylon to make a towel—the fibers are too smooth to hold much water, so liquid slips right off. That makes nylon good for raincoats, umbrellas, and tents.*

Nylon fibers are plastic threads squeezed out of a machine. That's why they look much smoother than fibers made by plants or animals.

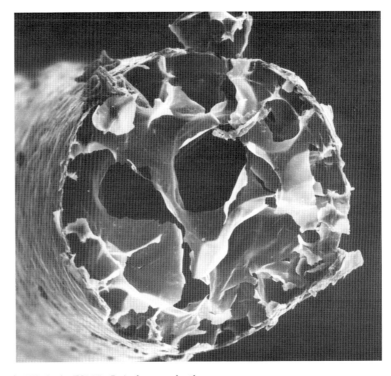

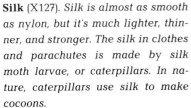

Silk (X127). *Silk is almost as smooth as nylon, but it's much lighter, thinner, and stronger. The silk in clothes and parachutes is made by silk moth larvae, or caterpillars. In nature, caterpillars use silk to make cocoons.*

Moth silk is similar to spider silk, but moths are much easier to raise than spiders. Silk moth caterpillars eat leaves and don't fight in a cage the way spiders would.

Nothing people have learned to make is stronger or more flexible, pound for pound, than the silk caterpillars have been making for millions of years.

Elk hair (X345). *Reindeer and other elk live where winters are long and cold. Their coats keep them warm enough to sleep in the snow. As you can see in this picture of an elk hair cut in half, the inside is hollow— trapping air and providing extra warmth, like the owl's feather.*

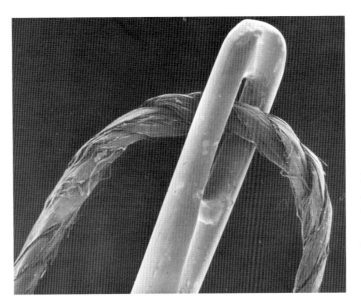

Polyester thread and needle (X23). *Like nylon, polyester fibers are machine-made and smooth.*

Even machine-made things come from natural sources, though. Polyester and nylon are plastics made from petroleum, ancient, crushed plants and animals.

FLEAS

Fleas are parasites; they live by sucking blood from other animals. Each species of flea usually bites a certain kind of animal, but fleas will bite different kinds of hosts if they get really hungry. People are sometimes bitten by cat fleas, for example.

Fleas look like they're wearing armor—and they are. Their cuticle has to be tough because their hosts are always trying to kill them.

Once fleas infest a house, they're hard to get rid of.

They can live for months without food and have a complex growth cycle, going from eggs to larvae to pupae to adults. Some bug sprays will kill adult fleas but not their eggs.

Like other bloodsucking animals, fleas can spread diseases, including one of the worst, bubonic plague. This plague, carried by rat fleas, killed millions of Europeans during the Middle Ages. Today the disease is rare and can be treated.

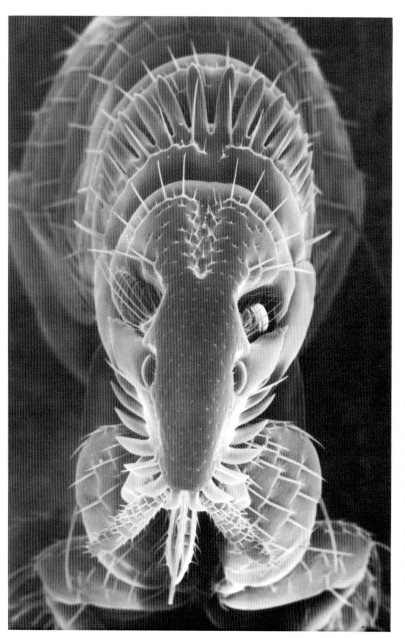

Cat flea (X180). *Fleas have poor eyesight. They probably see only light and dark, but that may be enough for them. They try to stay deep in the host's fur, where they can't be seen. Narrow bodies allow fleas to move quickly through hair.*

Before scientists invented insecticides, many people had fleas. Almost no one has human fleas anymore, but if you did you could get rid of them with a special shampoo.

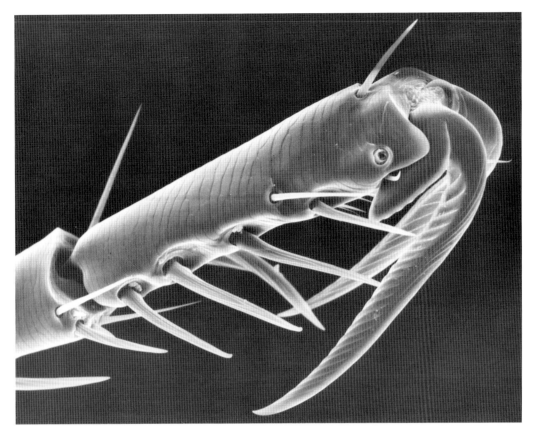

Cat flea claw (X690). *Backward-pointing claws and spines help fleas hang on to fur, even when the host is licking or scratching like crazy.*

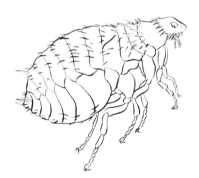

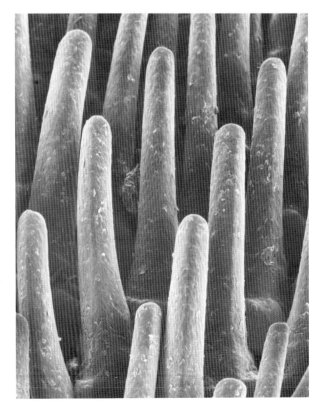

Cat tongue (X28). *Cats use their tongues to comb and clean their fur and to lap up milk and water. Looking at one through an SEM, you can see how it is also an effective tool against fleas.*

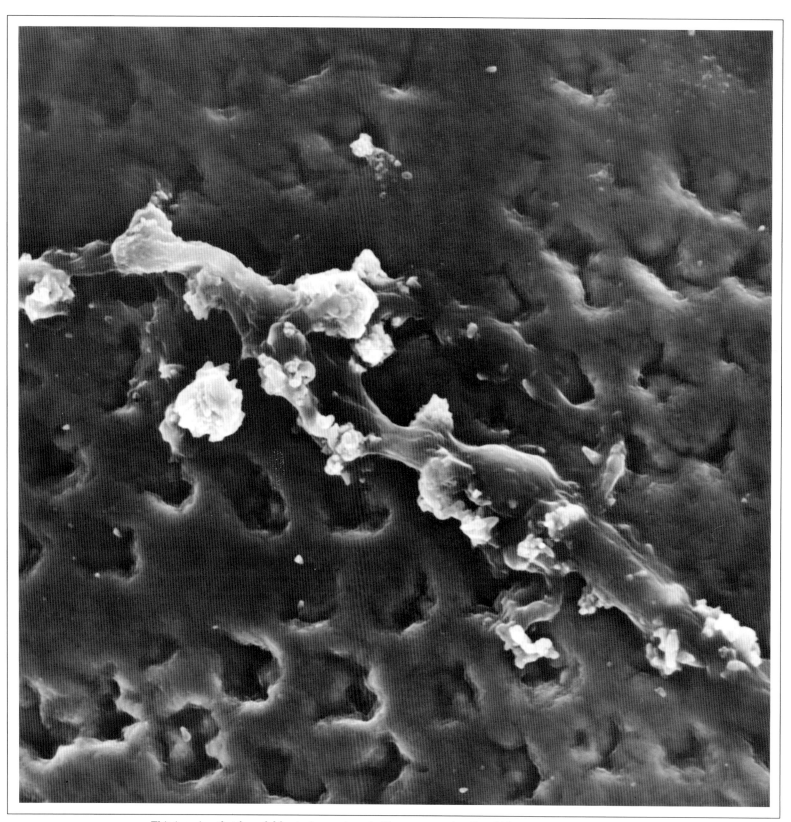

This is a sign that harmful bacteria are at work. How can you stop them? Turn to page 79 to find out.

WORLD FIVE

On You

People don't have hard shells like insects, but we are tough. Our skin, teeth, and hair keep moisture inside and invaders outside our bodies. But as tough as we are, we are still very sensitive to the world around us.

TONGUES and TASTE BUDS

Animals, including people, taste their food to know what they're eating and whether it's spoiled. We try to avoid things that look and smell like food but might make us sick.

We taste four basic flavors: sweet, sour, bitter, and salty. Taste cells are special skin cells grouped together in "buds" on our tongues. When we chew food and combine it with moisture in our mouth, some of the liquid gets into the pores of our taste buds. In split seconds, the taste buds communicate with each other, filtering and combining the chemical messages of flavor in complicated ways before sending taste signals to our brains. This communication and translation between taste cells gives foods thousands of distinct flavors.

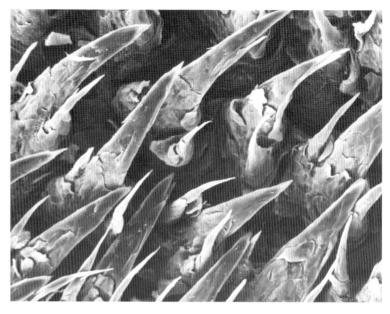

Guinea pig tongue (X275). *A guinea pig tongue feels rough to the touch — it works as a comb as well as a tongue.*

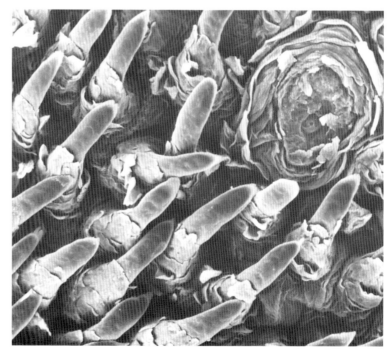

Rat tongue (X248). *You can see a taste bud in the upper right corner and a pore in the center of the bud where liquid can reach sensitive taste cells inside the bud. Rat tongues are rougher than ours, but their taste buds work the same way.*

Salt crystal (X306). *Salts are formed in chemical reactions in the laboratory and in nature. The round sodium ions and chloride ions that make up common table salt are packed tightly together to form cube-shaped crystals. No animal, including you, could survive without salt. We need small amounts for important chemical reactions in our bodies.*

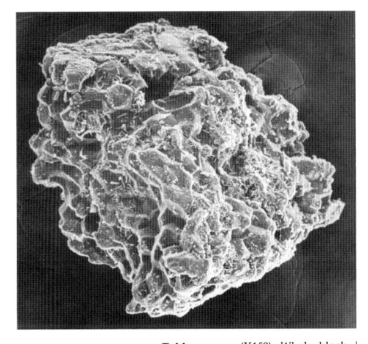

Table pepper (X152). *Whole black pepper is the dried fruit of a vine native to India. Pepper was one of the spices Europeans sailed around the world to find. On food, pepper is usually ground into bits like this one, releasing its flavor.*

Table sugar (X265). *Most table sugar comes from sugar cane, a kind of giant grass that grows in warm, wet climates. Plants use the energy of sunlight to convert carbon dioxide gas and water into sugar.*

All animals—people, birds, the smallest ants, and the largest whales —get energy from sugar.

SKIN

Your skin may not seem very special to you, but you couldn't live without it.

Your skin protects you from MicroAliens like bacteria and fungi. Most spiders can't bite through your skin—it's too tough. It's waterproof, too, and it holds in most of your moisture, so you don't dry out.

When you get hot, sweat glands in the skin release some water onto the surface. As the water evaporates, it carries heat away from your body.

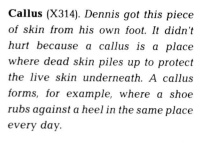

Callus (X314). *Dennis got this piece of skin from his own foot. It didn't hurt because a callus is a place where dead skin piles up to protect the live skin underneath. A callus forms, for example, where a shoe rubs against a heel in the same place every day.*

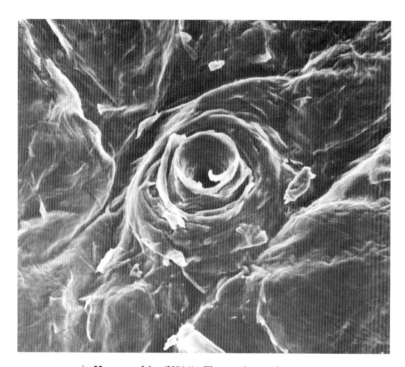

Human skin (X314). *The surface of our skin is dead—and it certainly looks that way in the picture.*

Dennis collected this dead skin from himself after his skin peeled from a sunburn. Skin cells are always dying, but too much sun kills more cells than usual.

As dead cells are rubbed off, living cells beneath the surface flatten out and take their places.

In this picture, you can see where a hair grew through the skin. The hair was left behind when the skin peeled away.

Skin fungus (X1,290). *Athlete's foot and other rashes are caused by this fungus. Fungi live everywhere, including on your skin, and usually don't cause problems. But if skin stays wet for too long, fungi may grow excessively, until they become irritating and cause itching.*

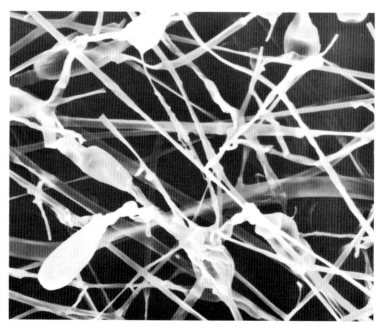

HAIR

The hair on all mammals, including you, isn't alive, but it is attached to living roots and nerve cells. That's why it hurts to have your hair pulled but not to have it cut.

Mammal hair has many purposes. Our bodies are almost entirely covered with hair, even when we're babies. It helps keep us warm in cold weather.

Fine hair helps make our skin feel soft. Rough hair on a man's face is a signal of gender and adulthood. Gray hair is often a sign of old age, on people and on other mammals.

Many mammals rely on hair color for camouflage. Some, like arctic foxes and snowshoe hares, even change their hair color as the seasons change—they're brown in summer and white in winter.

Cats and dogs have whiskers, special long hairs on their faces, to feel the world around them.

Mammals aren't the only creatures with hair. As we have seen, insects and spiders also use hairs for feeling and for camouflage.

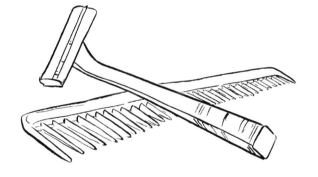

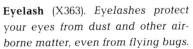

Human hair and comb (X25). *Hair has an outer "skin" called the cuticle. The scales of the cuticle overlap— their edges point toward the tip of the hair. That's why hair combs more easily away from your scalp—you don't brush against the stiff edges of the cuticle.*

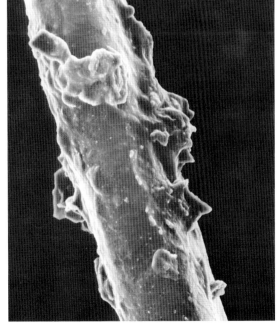

Eyelash (X363). *Eyelashes protect your eyes from dust and other airborne matter, even from flying bugs.*

Some people use mascara, a sticky black liquid, to make their lashes look thicker and darker. The lash in this picture is coated with mascara.

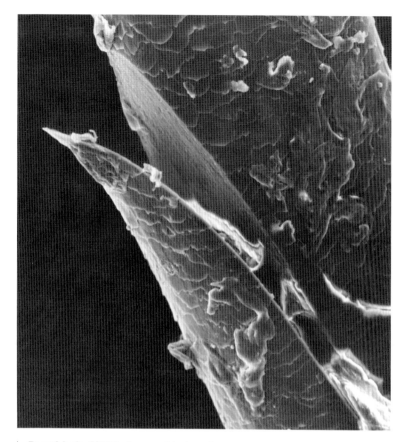

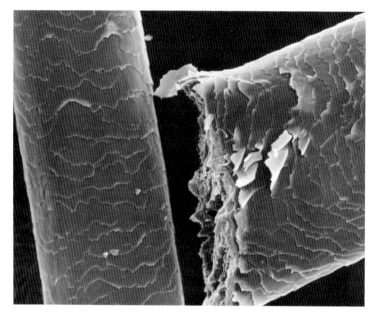

Hair cut with scissors (X539). *Scissors cut hair by squashing rather than slicing, and leave a more ragged end. An electric razor does the same thing. You can see the medulla, the soft inner part of the hair that has no color.*

Beard hair (X594). *A razor blade cut this hair cleanly. The blobs on the hair may be lotion or shaving cream. The light places on the edges of the cut are glowing because they've picked up an electrical charge from the microscope's electron beam.*

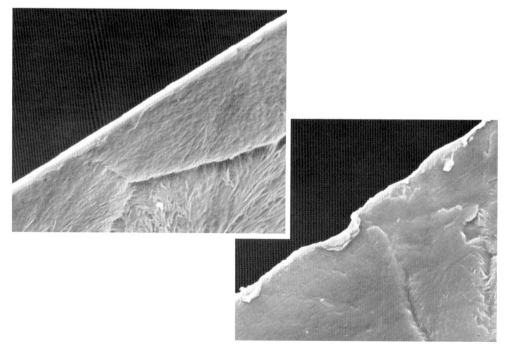

New (X2,300) **and used** (X1,610) **razor blades.** *Even a brand-new razor blade isn't perfectly sharp, but it's sharp enough to cut hair.*

As Dennis used it, the blade edge became worn and the sides smoother. Hair is stiff enough to dent the steel because the blade is so thin.

FINGERNAILS

Your fingernails are made from the same material as your hair. Like hair, they keep growing, so you have to cut them.

The claws, horns, and hooves of many animals are made of the same stuff. Rhino horns are actually made of very densely packed hairs.

Outside surface of a fingernail (X435). *Like hair, fingernails are not alive, but they are attached to sensitive skin and nerve cells.*

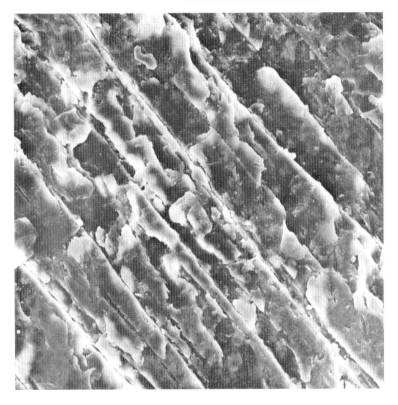

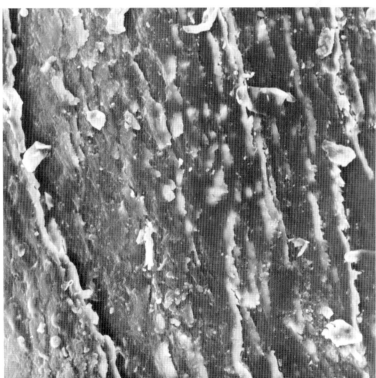

Inside surface of a fingernail (X435). *This is the inner surface near the edge of a nail, where dirt collects. You can see bits of skin and dust.*

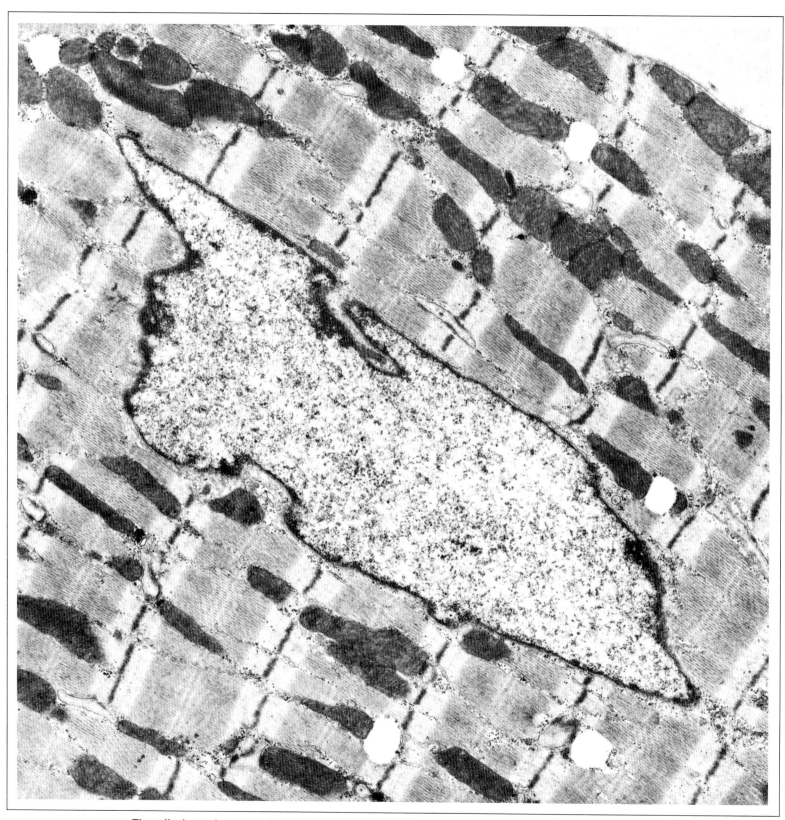

The cells that make up your body never take vacations. They spend their entire lives trying to keep you healthy.
Turn to page 79 to find out how.

WORLD SIX

Inside You

Inside your body are billions of microscopic workers, armies of microscopic soldiers, thousands of miles of passageways, and more electrical connections than in the most advanced computer. Even though we know more than ever about how our bodies work—thanks, in part, to the electron microscope—much of what goes on inside us is still a mystery.

CELLS

Every living thing is made of cells. Each cell is also a living thing, separate from the others, with a certain job to do. Every cell consumes nutrients, creates waste, and eventually dies.

Some creatures have only one cell. They are small, but you can see them under a visible-light microscope.

When the electron microscope was invented, scientists were able to look at cells more closely. They saw things they had never imagined.

You are a collection of about a hundred thousand billion cells working together. Cells look different from one another, but all of them, whether they're from an oak tree, a whale, an eagle, or your body, share the same basic structure.

Not all cells are microscopic. The largest cell known is the yolk of an ostrich egg. But the cells pictured here are small—so small that we used a transmission electron microscope (TEM), which shoots electrons *through* the sample instead of bouncing them *off* the sample. That's why these pictures look flatter and more two-dimensional than the others.

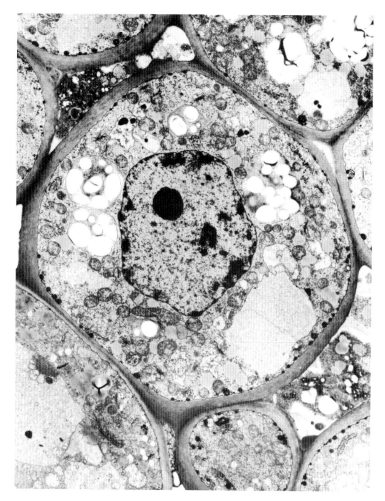

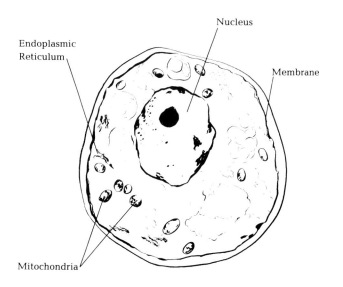

Endoplasmic Reticulum

Nucleus

Membrane

Mitochondria

Cell (X3,858). *Every cell has a skin, or membrane, separating it from other cells and from the outside world. Only certain molecules can pass through the membrane, such as food molecules, oxygen, carbon dioxide, and chemical messages. No one is sure exactly how the cell recognizes certain molecules and keeps others out.*

A cell combines nutrients such as fats and sugars with oxygen to create and store energy inside itself. Chemical messages from different parts of the body can tell the cell what to do and how to use that energy.

These cells are from a plant. They have very stiff walls so the plant can stand up without muscles or bones.

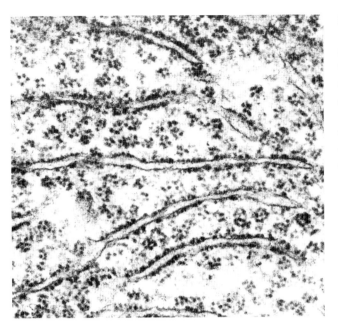

Endoplasmic reticulum (X52,326). *These ribbon-like structures in the cells of higher plants and animals were unknown before the invention of the electron microscope. The ER structures look like hollow hairs in this picture. Their purpose is still something of a mystery, but ribosomes, the tiny black dots, help to make new protein. The protein flows along the ER to where it is needed in the cell.*

Mitochondrion in a heart cell (X46,206). *Mitochondria are the powerhouses of a cell, allowing oxygen to be used to fuel the cell's biological engine. A single cell may have as many as ten thousand mitochondria.*

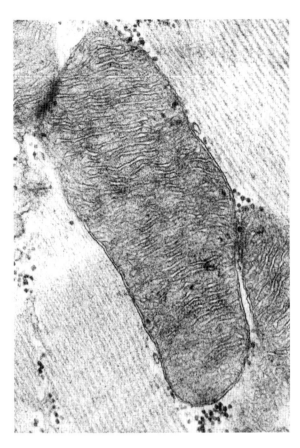

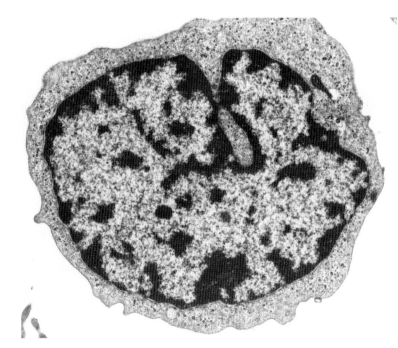

Neurons (X1,742). *Neurons are nerve cells that allow your body to communicate with your brain. They work together like circuits in a computer, sending messages back and forth.*

If you get close to a hot stove, for example, neurons in your skin will "fire," sending a message at about 2,000 miles per hour along a chain of neurons, through your spinal cord, to your brain: Hot! *Your brain will send a message back to your hand:* Don't touch!

Nucleus (X9,760). *Every cell contains a complicated genetic code, DNA, stored in chromosomes in the nucleus. It tells the cell how to grow, what its job is, and when to make a copy of itself.*

The code itself is copied when the cell divides, so each new cell contains identical information.

The chromosomes are spread out in this nucleus in what seems to be a random pattern. They look like dark blobs in this picture.

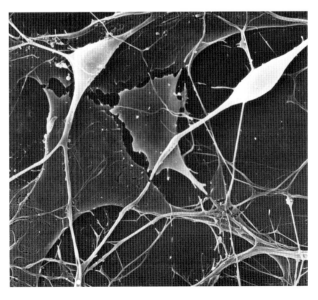

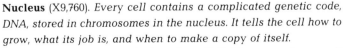

69

BLOOD

Blood is a mixture of cells, salts, minerals, and proteins, suspended in a liquid called plasma—which is mostly water.

Your blood has millions of red cells. They contain a protein called hemoglobin, which makes them red and "sticky" to oxygen and carbon dioxide. Red cells carry oxygen from your lungs to cells and, on their return to your lungs, carry some of the carbon dioxide to be expelled when you exhale.

For about every thousand red cells, your blood also contains a white cell. White cells are the guards, soldiers, and doctors of your bloodstream. Some of them hunt for debris and foreign invaders, including bacteria. When an invader is found, one kind of white cell surrounds it to prevent it from hurting you.

Other white cells rush to the site of an injury to help a scab form and close the wound. They can actually crawl across the wound and will die to protect you.

Your heart pumps blood through a network of passages, known as vessels, reaching all parts of your body, more than once every second—for every minute of your life. The blood system works even when you're asleep, supplying your body with energy, carrying chemical messages, and defending you from the outside world.

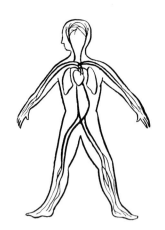

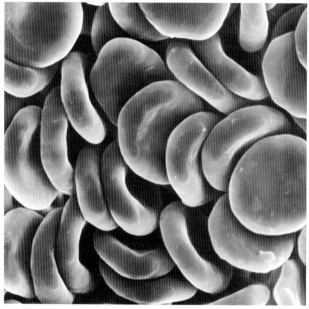

Red blood cells (X4,224). *Red cells are small: about a thousand would fit in the letter "o" in this book.*

Red cells are made in your bone marrow, the soft, dark interior of your bones. Each red cell lives for about four months. When it dies, it disintegrates and its chemical parts are recycled by your body.

All healthy red cells have one size and shape: a disk with dimples. This is apparently the best shape for carrying oxygen, the red cells' main job.

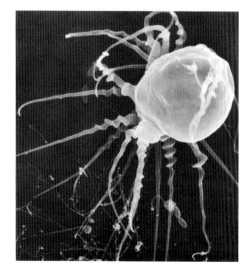

Macrophage (X2,904). *White cells have a variety of jobs, so their shapes and sizes vary. Many of them look like blobs. This white cell, a macrophage from the lung, is engulfing, or phagocytosing, bacteria.*

Once the bacteria are enveloped, they are destroyed by chemicals inside the macrophage.

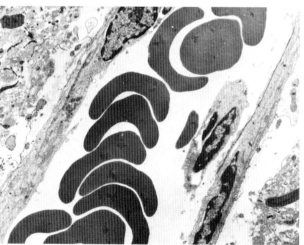

Red cells in a blood vessel (X4,184). *Red cells are wider than some of the blood vessels they travel through, so the cells have to stretch and squeeze to fit. That's how they're able to supply the other cells in your body with oxygen.*

This picture was taken with a TEM, which scientists use to look inside cells.

LUNGS

The lungs of all mammals are like sponges. We breathe through a single passage in our throats that divides into two passageways, then into four, eight, sixteen, and so on, until the passages become so small they are microscopic. They lead to microscopic air sacs whose walls are much thinner and more delicate than paper.

On the other side of these sacs are blood vessels. The walls of the sacs are so thin that air can pass through. When red blood cells arrive at the sacs, they release their loads of carbon dioxide. The gas passes through the walls of the sacs and into your lungs.

Oxygen and other gases pass the other way and "stick" to the red cells.

Certain gases that are not good for you, such as carbon monoxide, can pass through the walls of the sacs. Carbon monoxide is produced by cigarettes and car engines, among other things. The gas "sticks" to red cells more powerfully than oxygen. If a person inhales too much carbon monoxide at one time, red cells "fill up" with it and lose their ability to carry oxygen to the body's cells. Without oxygen, the cells will die. If too many cells die at one time, the person will die, too.

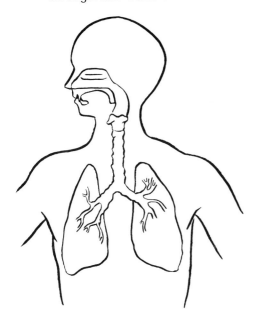

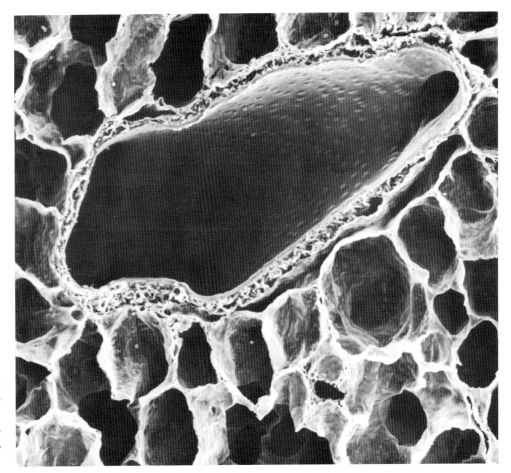

Lung tissue (X221). *This small cross section of a rabbit's lung shows the tiny sacs called alveoli where oxygen enters the blood. The membranes that form the alveoli are so thin that oxygen and carbon dioxide can pass right through.*

In the center, you can see a large passageway for air that supplies the alveoli.

VIRUSES

A virus is a chain of molecules smaller than the smallest bacterium. A virus doesn't breathe or consume nutrients such as food, water, or air, and can't grow on its own. It reproduces by invading a living cell and using the cell's parts and biological machinery to copy itself.

Viruses can infect every life form—even plants and bacteria. In the last fifty years, science has eliminated the threat posed by many dangerous viruses with vaccines, medicines that prevent viral infections. Smallpox, polio, and measles, for example, are viral diseases that used to claim millions of lives. Today, we are vaccinated with altered viruses that don't make us sick. Once our bodies learn to recognize the viruses, our immune systems can defend us against real infections. Some viruses, such as the flu, constantly change, however, so scientists have trouble making reliable vaccines for them.

Eventually new vaccines will be developed to prevent other viral infections—maybe even AIDS and some kinds of cancer.

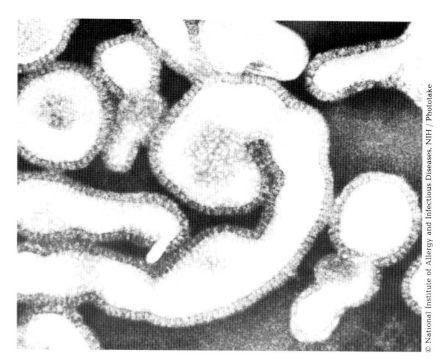

Influenza A virus (X133,400). *Influenza, the flu, is caused by a virus in people. You can catch the flu when you inhale tiny droplets from the cough or sneeze of an infected person, or when you get droplets on your hands and then touch your eyes, nose, or mouth.*

Once inside your body, the flu virus takes over the operations of some cells to build more virus particles. Eventually the infected cells die, and new virus particles move out to attack other cells.

Your immune system responds to help you. One response is to manufacture antibodies to neutralize the virus. After a week or so, your body will usually defeat the invader and you'll feel better. Once you have caught a certain strain of flu, your body will recognize it if you are exposed to it again, and the antibodies will destroy it, preventing another illness.

Some people may take a flu vaccine containing an altered virus that doesn't make them sick. The vaccine stimulates their immune system to make antibodies that will recognize the invading virus and prevent an infection.

Tobacco mosaic virus (X87,142). *The rod-shaped particles in this picture are a virus that kills tobacco plants. Like other viruses, this one has a coating of protein, which protects it from the outside world and the defenses of the host it attacks.*

When a Russian scientist named Dimitry Ivanovsky first proved the existence of a virus in 1892, he used the tobacco mosaic virus, but he could not see it. When the electron microscope was invented in Germany forty years later, the virus scientists looked for was the tobacco mosaic. It was the first virus ever seen.

Today, more than sixty years later, viruses are still mysterious. We have developed vaccines to prevent some infections, but it's still hard to stop a virus after it has infected the cell without killing the cell itself.

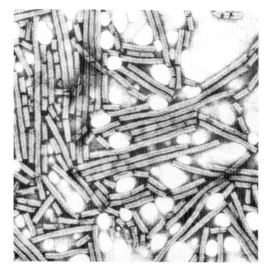

CILIA

Some of the simplest creatures have cilia, tiny arms they use to swim through the water where they live. Some one-celled animals swim by moving their cilia in a motion like a backstroke.

Larger animals, including some worms and larvae, move through the water by waving thousands of cilia together.

You have millions of cilia in your body. Beating in waves, they push foreign particles out of your lungs, nose, and ears. They move fluids through your brain, intestines, and reproductive tract.

Cilia are one of the many things you have in common with microscopic animals.

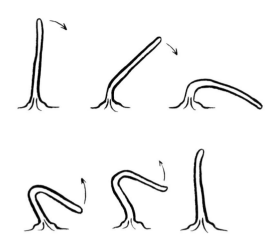

Brain cilia (X6,424). *These tufts of cilia move fluids along the brain's folded surfaces.*

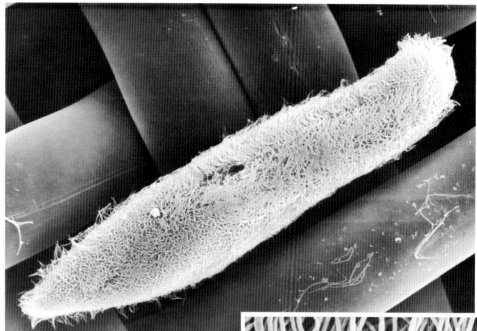

Paramecium (X641). *This microscopic one-celled animal, a kind of protozoan, moves through the water by waving its cilia in unison. You can find animals like these in lakes, rivers, and oceans around the world.*

In the background is a micropore nylon screen Dennis used to strain the paramecium out of water.

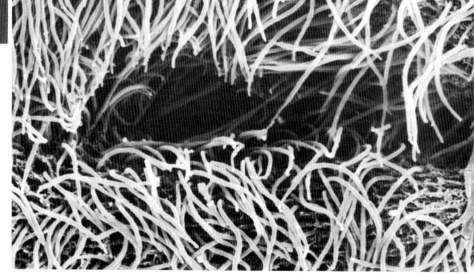

Paramecium gullet (X5,247). *The paramecium also uses cilia to wave particles of food into its mouth, or gullet.*

INTESTINES

Stretched out, your intestinal tract would be about five times as long as you are tall.

The inner surface of part of your intestine is covered with millions of villi, microscopic fingers that make the intestinal wall look like velvet. Villi increase the food-collecting surface area of your intestine, giving it about a thousand square feet of area.

The electron microscope showed scientists that each villus is covered with microvilli, which increase the intestinal surface area even more.

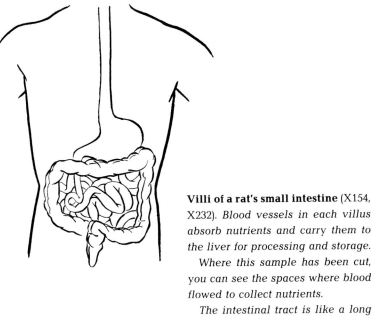

Villi of a rat's small intestine (X154, X232). *Blood vessels in each villus absorb nutrients and carry them to the liver for processing and storage.*

Where this sample has been cut, you can see the spaces where blood flowed to collect nutrients.

The intestinal tract is like a long tube with a muscular coat which pumps food along its length.

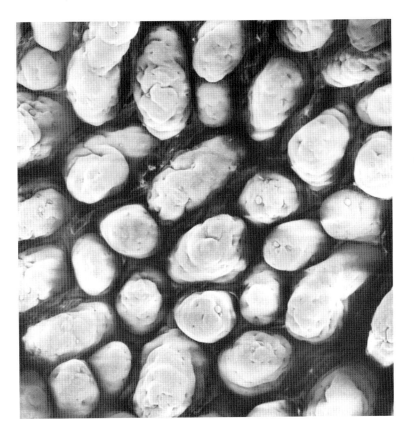

Mystery Photo Answers

Acknowledgments

Further Study

Mystery Photo Answers

Frontispiece

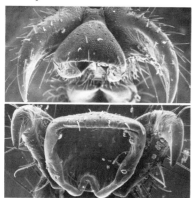

Walking stick claw and suction cup (X150, X172). *Suction cups are an important part of a walking stick's disguise. By seeming to grow from a branch—instead of wrapping claws around it—the insect looks more like a twig.*

Page 24

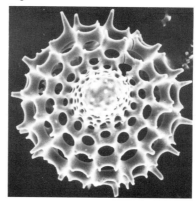

Radiolarian (X1,199). *This is a test, a shell-like skeleton, from a one-celled animal known as a protozoan. It once had arms, pseudopodia, that reached through the holes to help it move through the water and grab food particles.*

Living outside its mineral cage, this protozoan would have been an easy meal for almost any animal. But inside its sharp skeleton, the radiolarian would have been much harder to eat.

Page 8

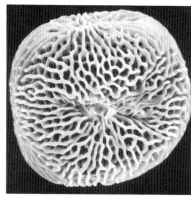

Pollen grain from a geranium flower (X3,133). *The pollen's secret message—its genetic code—will pass through the aperture, or slot, in the center of the grain after it lands on the stigma, the sticky surface on the female part of the flower.*

Once it has the pollen's code, the flower will be able to make a new seed.

The pollen grain is strong and light and coated with a gummy film to help it stick to an insect's body.

Page 34

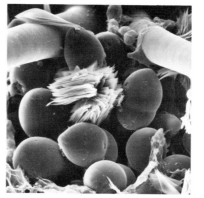

Insect eggs on a grape leaf (X2,178). *A mother insect protected her eggs with sharp crystals—breathing or eating these crystals could be fatal to another insect. The baby insects, larvae, will probably eat the grape leaf when they emerge from their eggs. We don't know how they avoid being hurt by their mother's crystals.*

Page 46

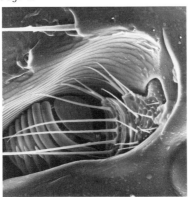

Cat flea's antenna (X1,439). *A flea faces constant attack from its host—in this case, a cat. The flea needs armor to survive the cat's claws and rough tongue. The insect's sensitive antennae are recessed, like your eardrums, to protect them from injury.*

Page 66

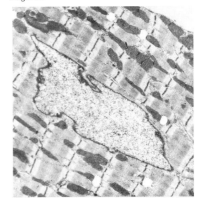

Heart muscle cell (X16,940). *The gray area in the center of the picture is the nucleus containing the code that controls the cell's function and reproduction.*

The rest of the cell is mostly tiny, muscle-like fibers. Heart cells contract in unison to make the heart beat and pump blood.

The dark spots are mitochondria, where the cell's energy is made.

The cell collects nutrients and oxygen through the bloodstream. If the bloodstream is blocked—by deposits of fat, for example—cells will eventually die from a lack of oxygen and nutrients.

Page 58

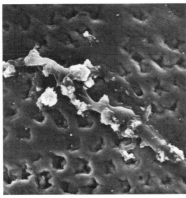

Tooth with tartar (X3,630). *Teeth may seem smooth, but you can see from this picture that their surfaces are porous and rough enough for things to stick to them.*

Bacteria stick to your teeth and produce a substance that reacts with chemicals in your saliva to produce tartar. It has formed on this tooth. Tartar between teeth and gums can irritate the gums, cause an infection, and eventually damage the tooth.

Brushing will help keep tartar from forming, but once it does form, you must go to the dentist to have it scraped off.

ACKNOWLEDGMENTS

Many people and sources of information helped us complete this book.

The books and staff at the American Museum of Natural History library were particularly helpful.

Thanks also to Louis Sorkin at the museum for advice, expertise, water bugs, whirligigs, and dragonflies; to Diane Cole at the Long Island Game Park for elk hair; to Cal Welbourne at Ohio State University for dust mites; to the staff of the University of Washington, including Joe Wilmhoff for colorization of micrographs, Dr. Jon Kott and family for assorted specimens, Rod Crawford for moths, Doug Ewing for botanical specimens, Barbara Reine for foraminiferan and radiolarian specimens, Dr. Dan Luchtel for lung specimens, Ellie Duffield for botanical specimens, Mary Bicknell for microbiology specimens, and Dr. Edward Haskins for his expertise and library; to Carla Stehr of the Northwest Fisheries Center for fish specimens; to the National Institute of Allergy and Infectious Diseases, NIH / Phototake for use of the Influenza A micrograph; to Kerry Ruef and David Melody for walking sticks, expertise, and for sharing *The Private Eye*; to Ramon and Micki Bladuell for tropical specimens; to Dr. Wendy Berkowitz for her expertise and comments; to Professor William Pardee of Cornell University for expertise; to Dixie J. Knabe of Seven Hills–Lotspeich School of Cincinnati for expertise and comments; and to Mr. and Mrs. Edwin Kunkel for a variety of specimens.

Special thanks to our editor, Wes Adams, for his patience and diligence.

FURTHER STUDY

To learn more about microscopes, plants, insects, people, or anything else in this book, visit your library.

To find out about all kinds of animals, we return again and again to *Grzimek's Animal Life Encyclopedia*, edited by Bernhard Grzimek (New York: Van Nostrand Reinhold, 1984).

Good books about the microscopic world include *The Secret Garden* by David Bodanis (New York: Simon & Schuster, 1992), *Scanning Nature* by D. Claugher (London: British Museum, 1983), *Living Images* by Gene Shih and Richard Kessel (Boston: Science Books International, 1982), and *Under the Microscope: A Hidden World Revealed* by Jeremy Burgess, Michael Marten, and Rosemary Taylor (New York: Cambridge University Press, 1990).